THE VICTIMS RETURN

Survivors of the Gulag After Stalin

Stephen F. Cohen

PublishingWorks
Exeter, NH
2010

PublishingWorks, Inc.
151 Epping Road
Exeter, NH 03833
603-778-9883

603-772-7200
www.PublishingWorks.com

Distributed to the trade by Publishers Group West

Designed by Anna Pearlman

LCCN: 2009927779
ISBN-13: 978-1-935557-40-8

Printed on recycled paper.

*In loving memory
of Anna Mikhailovna Larina (1914–1996),
who lost her husband, infant son, and more than twenty years
of her life to Stalin's terror, but never her humanity.*

It can't be covered up. People will come out of prison, return to their native places, tell their relatives and friends and acquaintances what actually happened . . . that those who remained alive had been innocent victims of repression.

—Nikita Khrushchev

The return of so many people from prison and exile is a great historic turning point. The scale on which the dead have come back to life is difficult to imagine.

—Svetlana Alliluyeva (Stalin's daughter)

Contents

—⟋⟍—

—⟋⟍—

Prologue

The mass terror carried out by Stalin and his closest associates in the 1930s, 1940s, and early 1950s was the cruelest not only in the history of the people of our country but of the entire civilized world . . . A monstrous machine was created for the destruction of completely innocent people.

—A Soviet Journal, 1989

I want to name them all by name,
But the list was taken and is nowhere to be found.

—Anna Akhmatova, *Requiem*

Joseph Stalin's reign of terror in the Soviet Union has been called "the other holocaust," and with good reason. During its twenty-four-year history, more innocent men, women, and children perished than died in Hitler's destruction of the European Jews.

Contrary to the myth that the terror struck mainly high echelons of the Soviet system, no segment of society was spared. Old Bolsheviks, as the Leninist founding leaders were known, fell victim, as did Stalin's own appointees, lowly young Communists, and priests. Party, state, and military officials were swept away, but often so were their secretaries, drivers, and housekeepers. Famous performers, writers, and scientists were "taken," an expression widely heard at the time, but so too were millions of peasants and workers. In many cases, a victim's immediate and extended family relatives were also arrested. In the end, the great majority of Stalin's victims, 70 percent or more, were "ordinary" citizens, not members of the Communist Party or any other Soviet elite.[1]

Stalin's mass terror began in the years from 1929 to 1933 with the ruthless methods he used in the countryside—armed force, often fatal deportations of entire families, and wide-spread famine—to collectivize the nation's 125 million peasants. From 1936 to 1939, his bloody repressions descended on Moscow, Leningrad, and virtually every other Soviet city in what became known as The Great Terror. Over seventeen months in 1937 and 1938 alone, 1.7 million people were arrested, more than 700,000 of them shot, and another 300,000 to 400,000 sent into punishing exile in Siberia, Kazakhstan, and other far-away places.

The number of arrests diminished in 1939, but did not end, neither during nor after the epic Soviet war against Nazi Germany from 1941 to 1945. During the war, entire small nationalities, totaling some 2.5 million people, were forcibly deported from their Soviet homelands in brutal conditions that left many of them dead or dying. Following the wartime victory, a million or more repatriated Soviet prisoners of war and still other small nationalities were sent to Stalin's own concentration camps or to penal settlements. And in the late 1940s and early 1950s, a new wave of mass repressions unfolded in the cities, including an anti-Jewish pogrom, which threatened to replicate those of the late 1930s. Stalin's terror ended only when its creator and master finally died on March 5, 1953.

How many Soviet citizens perished in the terror is still a matter of dispute, even among specialists and even after considerable (but not full) access to long secret archives. Leaving aside the nation's 26.5 million war deaths, considered estimates range from 12 to 20 million during Stalin's rule from 1929 to 1953. Those estimates include deaths caused by collectivization and the mass deportations.

Many victims, summarily tried and sentenced to death by assembly-line tribunals known as "troikas" or tortured to death, did not survive the initial stage of arrest and "interrogation" in prison. While the numbers were still manageable, most were shot in the back of the head and buried in existing cemeteries or cremated. As the volume of victims grew, so did mass killing areas and graves around the country. They are still being uncovered in the twenty-first century.

The great majority of those who survived or bypassed the prisons were dispatched to the Gulag Archipelago, as Aleksandr Solzhenitsyn famously named Stalin's vast system of jails, transit, forced labor camps, "special settlements," and other forms of harsh internal exile. The total number of Gulag inmates—or zeks, as they were commonly called, from the Russian word for prisoner (*zaklyuchyonnyi*)—during the Stalin era also is unknown. The figures, 12 to 14 million, now used by some specialists, may be a conservative estimate.

Millions of these inmates never returned from the Gulag. A very large percent of forced-labor zeks were turned into "camp dust" by crushing work, brutal guards, malnutrition, and extreme climates. This was especially true in the large clusters of mining and lumber camps known by their remote regions in the Soviet Arctic and Far East. Among the most notorious were Vorkuta, Norilsk, and especially Kolyma, which included the outlying Gulag capital city of Magadan. In one camp alone, 3,372 zeks died in a period of six months.[2]

How the number of victims grew so large is horrifying to consider but not hard to explain. As with all such episodes of massive evil, the terror involved complicity from the highest levels of the system to the lowest. Stalin, abetted by a small group of men around him at the top of the Soviet Communist Party and state, personally initiated and directed the terror. He issued general directives, signed lists of thousands of individuals to be arrested and shot, and set quotas for the number of "enemies of the people" to be found in cities and institutions across the enormous country.

A million or more political police officials, known in the 1930s and 1940s as the NKVD, implemented those orders, often competing to over-fulfill the quotas. Headed by two of Stalin's political creatures—a tiny, bi-sexual, drug-addicted fanatic, Nikolai Yezhov, and then by a kind of personification of evil, Lavrenti Beria—the NKVD arrested, interrogated, shot, transported, and guarded the victims. Lower down, millions of other Soviet citizens fed the terror by denouncing their co-workers, acquaintances, friends, and even relatives. They did so out of ideological zealotry, fear, personal resentments and ambitions, and other pathologies that always emerge in such times.

But it was the conspiratorial theory behind the terror, formulated by Stalin and promoted into a national mania, which systematically multiplied the number of victims. According to Stalinist ideology, the country was full of covert enemies posing as loyal citizens—assassins, saboteurs, and traitors—who were conspiring to destroy the Soviet system and betray the nation to foreign powers. By definition, and in law, conspiracy requires more than a lone perpetrator. For every individual arrested, the NKVD therefore had to find co-conspirators guilty of "counter-revolutionary" crimes punishable under the infamous Article 58 of the Criminal Code. Unless otherwise specified, interrogators seemed to have operated on the premise of five to ten accomplices. Ten arrests could thereby lead to a hundred; hundreds to thousands; and thousands to millions.

Because very few such conspiracies actually existed, if any, citizens who were arrested were forced to give false confessions and the names of other innocent people, usually beginning with career associates, relatives, and friends. Isolated, shocked, and afraid, some victims quickly succumbed to threats, sleep deprivation, and psychological pressure—"vegetarian methods," as survivors termed them—but a great many were so brutally tortured, which Stalin personally authorized and encouraged, they were unable to stand. A remarkable number held out until they died or until over-burdened prison officials turned to other cases. To escape more torture, some victims managed to commit suicide in their cells.

Most, however, were eventually broken by unrelenting physical pain. Here, for example, is the agonized plea of the renowned theater director Vsevolod Meyerhold, written in his cell and sent to a leader close to Stalin:

> They began to beat me—a sick, sixty-five-year-old man. They made me lie face-down and beat the soles of my feet and my spine with a braided rubber whip. Then they sat me on a chair and beat my legs from above with great force. In the days that followed, when those parts of my legs were covered with extensive internal hemorrhaging, they beat the red, blue, and yellow bruises again with the whip. The pain was so intense it felt like boiling water was being poured on these sensitive areas. I shouted and cried from the pain. They beat my back with the same rubber whip and punched my face from above with their fists ... Death, I told myself, is easier to bear than this. I began to slander myself in the hope it would lead quickly to the scaffold.[3]

Extracting so many false confessions and innocent names also required even more extreme methods. Women were sexually brutalized, a young actress being repeatedly violated with truncheons. A Red Army commander, Marshal Vasily Blyukher, was beaten so badly one eye dangled from its socket, and then was beaten more until he died. Some prisoners were mutilated, their ears and noses cut off. And ultimately there were threats to subject the victim's family members to the same treatment. Audible cries of women being tortured in the prison and a decree authorizing the death penalty for children as young as twelve made the threats credible. Indeed, some husbands and wives were tortured in the other's presence, as were their young children, and forced to watch their teenage daughters being raped. When finally brought before a troika, many unfortunates found the courage to retract their testimonies, as did Meyerhold. They were shot anyway, usually within a few minutes, though in some cases not before again being brutally beaten.[4]

Thick "martyrologies" have been compiled in cities across Russia and other former Soviet republics for more than twenty years, but the names of all those who died in the terror, and thus the total number, can never be known. Not even archives—repositories of factual but also fragmentary and falsified documents—hold the answer. Too many victims simply disappeared. "People vanished," Stalin's own daughter later recalled, "like shadows in the night."[5] Readers who know Boris Pasternak's celebrated novel *Doctor Zhivago*, or the popular film based on it, may remember, at the end, Pasternak's casual explanation of the fate of his beloved Lara:

> One day Larisa Fyodorovna went out and never came back. She must have been arrested in the street, as happened in those days. She vanished without a trace and probably died somewhere, forgotten as a nameless number on a list that afterward got mislaid, in one of the innumerable mixed or women's camps in the north.

Interviewing victims for this book about the few million people who somehow survived Stalin's torture prisons and labor camps, I was constantly reminded not to forget the many more millions who did not return. Nor should my readers.

CHAPTER 1

The History of A Book

Every era gives rise to its own specific types of sources.

—Vladlen Loginov (Russian historian)

I advise you to stop spending time with people who have grievances against the Soviet government.

—A KGB officer to this author, 1981

Influenced by centuries of repression and censorship, Russian writers often say that manuscripts, like people, have their own histories. Certainly, it is true of this book. I drafted a summary of the project almost thirty years ago, in 1983. Until recently, it remained, along with the large amount of materials I had collected, in my files. But the subject never ceased to be an important part of my long professional and personal relationship with Russia, as readers will soon understand.

The project was intended to be, as much of it still is, the story of survivors of Stalin's Gulag who returned to Soviet society under his successor, Nikita Khrushchev, in the years from 1953 to 1964. I did the original research in Moscow in the repressive late 1970s and early 1980s, when public discussion of Stalin's terror and its victims was officially banned and often punished inside the Soviet Union. No sensible scholar—I was a professor at Princeton University—normally would have chosen a subject for which so little information was readily available. But, I came to think, the subject chose me.

It began even earlier, though only as an afterthought. In 1965, I was walking in a London park with the writer Robert Conquest while discussing his new undertaking, which became the famous and indispensable book, *The Great Terror*. Conquest, who had recently befriended me, was already an eminent Anglo-American man-of-letters—a poet, novelist, literary critic, and political historian. I, more than twenty years younger, had no writerly achievements at all, only the beginnings of a Ph.D. dissertation on Nikolai Bukharin, a Soviet founding leader put on trial and executed by Stalin in 1938 as an "enemy of the people."

Because my work on Bukharin, who was remembered at that time mainly as the model for Arthur Koestler's famous novel about the Moscow Show Trials, *Darkness at Noon*, eventually led to this book, I should explain why I chose him as a subject. It was not due, as some people later thought, to any family ties to the Soviet experience. (I grew up remote from all of that, in Kentucky.) Instead, my graduate studies suggested that Bukharin's ideas, not Leon Trotsky's, as was generally believed, had been the real Soviet alternative to Stalinism. I had in mind the market-related, evolutionary New Economic Policy, or NEP, introduced by Lenin in 1921 and elaborated on and defended by Bukharin after Lenin's death in 1924. His ouster from the leadership by Stalin in 1929 led to the brutal collectivization of the peasantry and thus, I thought, to the terror.

Little more than that reinterpretation of the NEP 1920s was on my mind in 1965. But listening to Conquest discuss new materials he had found on the 1930s, I remarked, as an aside, that I had learned Bukharin's widow, Anna Larina, and their son, Yuri Larin, had somehow survived Stalin's terror and were alive somewhere in Moscow. Twenty-six years younger than her husband, Anna had endured more than two decades in prisons, labor camps, and Siberian exile, while Yuri, separated from his mother at barely a year old, had grown up in an orphanage without knowing his parents' identity. (Larina later told their story in her memoirs, *This I Cannot Forget*.)[1] Yes, Conquest replied, no doubt there were still millions of such survivors all over the Soviet Union. We wondered, very briefly, what their lives had been like after the Gulag.

The seed was planted, but it grew only later. In 1976, I began living in Moscow for extended periods, usually on a U.S.-Soviet academic exchange program. By then, my book about Bukharin had been published in New York and a smuggled copy had made its way to Anna Larina and Yuri, who welcomed me into their family.[2] Indeed, much of my Moscow social life was shaped by the extended Bukharin family, which included Anna's two other children, Nadezhda and Mikhail, born in Siberian exile, with her second husband, Fyodor Fadeyev, whom she met in the Gulag and who died shortly after their return to Moscow in 1959.

I soon realized that most of the people I came to know through the Bukharin family were also survivors of Stalin's terror or relatives of his other victims. Public knowledge of their terrible ordeal had been heavily censored since shortly after Khrushchev's overthrow in 1964, and they had little hope, if any, of ever making it widely known. For that reason, and because of my "adopted-son" relationship with Anna Larina, the ranking old Bolshevik widow in those martyred circles, they were eager to tell me their stories and give me unpublished memoirs. Suddenly and unexpectedly, I found myself dwelling in a subterranean history, a kind of living archaeological find, known only fragmentarily in the Soviet Union and almost not at all in the West. Writing that history, it seemed, had fallen to me.

—∿—

The book I originally planned had two purposes. Using what I had learned from doing a biography of Bukharin, I wanted to write a collective biography of Gulag returnees, beginning with their liberation in the 1950s and ending with their efforts to rejoin society and salvage what remained of their lives. The second purpose reflected my interest in reform in the Soviet system. Repressed historical traditions, as the NEP 1920s and Bukharin's ideas then were, had often led elsewhere to major political changes. Even in the ultra-conservative Soviet 1970s, I thought it was also likely to happen, at least eventually, in Moscow. In that connection, I wanted to examine how the return of millions of Gulag zeks after Stalin's death had affected policymaking and the system itself under Khrushchev.

This second purpose was outside the mainstream of Western studies. Still adhering to the "totalitarianism" model, most studies treated the Soviet political system as something apart from both its history and society, largely unaffected by either and thus essentially unreformable.[3] The impact of Gulag returnees in the 1950s and 1960s seemed to suggest otherwise. Their fates were a central factor in the intensely historicized politics of the period, when controversies over the past became an inescapable aspect of current struggles over power and policy at the top. At the same time, the personal needs of so many freed prisoners and their families created both a social constituency below for further de-Stalinization from above and a test of the system's capacity for change. (Before it became widespread in Western Soviet studies, I was trying to fuse social and political history.)

But where could I obtain the information needed for such a highly empirical work? Almost no secondary literature existed on the subject; the best Western books about the terror, notably Conquest's, focused on people's victimization, not their subsequent experiences.[4] And in a country of encompassing censorship, closed archives, still-intimidated victims, and a hostile state, there was, not surprisingly, only one fragmentary study of returnees written by a Soviet author—the brief account of several post-Gulag lives at the end of the third volume of Aleksandr Solzhenitsyn's epic work, *The Gulag Archipelago*, which appeared in the West in the 1970s.[5]

This meant I had to rely mainly on primary or first-hand accounts. Memoirs would have been ideal, but there were scarcely any. A number of uncensored Gulag memoirs had been published abroad over the years but were of limited value for my purpose. Most covered the period before Stalin's death or said almost nothing about life after the Gulag. And some were written by repatriated foreign prisoners, including a few Americans who had gone to the Soviet Union in the 1930s in search of work or the promised land, whose experiences were not sufficiently representative of Soviet ones.[6]

There were only two exceptions. One was Solzhenitsyn's own idiosyncratic memoir, issued in English as *The Oak and The Calf*, which dealt largely with his struggle, before being deported in 1974, to publish his writings in the Soviet Union, not his personal life. More valuable were the two-volume memoirs of the former Communist teacher Eugenia Ginzburg, *Journey Into the Whirlwind* and *Within the Whirlwind*, which remain essential reading on the Stalinist terror years. (In 2009, parts of them were made into a British theatrical film.) In particular, Ginzburg's second volume recounts her life after being released from camp in the late 1940s, including her forced residence in Magadan, where she tutored children of NKVD officers and where her own young son was able to rejoin her.

There were, however, two other sources of written information, both of them Soviet, little known, and important. One included revelations about the terror published in the Soviet Union during the somewhat relaxed censorship of Khrushchev's "Thaw," as his de-Stalinizing policies became known. The widespread impression, even among specialists, that few such writings were actually permitted even at that time—in literature, for example, only Solzhenitsyn's famous short novel, *One Day in the Life of Ivan Denisovich*—or that they were unworthy of attention because they were pro-Soviet, is mistaken. (Varlam Shalamov, regarded by some as the greatest Gulag writer, refused to be so dismissive of those more conformist authors.)[7]

In the early and mid-1960s, many informative commentaries on Stalin's terror, including memoir accounts by Gulag survivors, appeared in officially sanctioned Soviet publications, some thinly disguised as fiction. This was the case not only in Moscow and Leningrad, but in less cosmopolitan cities as well. Prompted by returnees who advised me in various ways, I found valuable information in literary-political journals edited and published in remote regions where there had been large concentrations of camp inmates and exiles, and where many had remained after their release, particularly in Siberia and Kazakhstan. Getting access to those journals was difficult, but well worth the effort.[8]

The other written Soviet source of information was entirely uncensored: a growing volume of typescript materials circulated by hand and known as *samizdat*, or "self-published." Those expressions of unofficial glasnost—a word later adopted by Mikhail Gorbachev to denote his policy of ending censorship—produced an array of writings ranging from histories, memoirs, and fiction to contemporary political and social commentary.[9] Not surprisingly, terror-era subjects and survivor-authors themselves were a major component of this new and essential literature.

Most of all, though, I relied on the personal testimonies of Stalin's victims whom I came to know. In the beginning, I met them through the Bukharin family, but soon also through three other exceptional Muscovites. Two were well-known dissident historians, as well as terror victims, with whom I developed close personal and professional relations over the years, Roy Medvedev and Anton Antonov-Ovseyenko.[10]

Then in his early fifties, Roy, whose father, an army officer and Communist professor of philosophy, had perished in the Gulag, was a unique figure in dissident circles, not only because he combined Marxist-Leninist views with pro-democracy ones. An academic by education and political loner by nature, his greatest achievement at the time was the first authentic history of Stalinism ever written inside the Soviet Union, *Let History Judge*, though publishable only abroad. It remains a powerful indictment and indispensable source of information.

Unlike many dissidents, Roy, who had joined the Communist Party after his father's exoneration in 1956 and had been expelled in 1969, was coolly analytical and valued facts over polemics, rarely expressing disagreement in more than a bemused smile. Tall, handsome, and slightly stooped, he had the silver-haired appearance of a British don, enhanced by clothes from his twin brother, Zhores, a scientist living in exile in London due to his own protest activities. Roy and I became friends, but our frequent discussions were usually those of academic colleagues. He had knowledge I needed about historical events, people, and materials; I knew the Western literature that he did not. It was, we agreed, an excellent collaboration.[11]

Anton was also a loner with historical interests similar to Roy's, but otherwise the two men were very different. Both of Anton's parents, including his father, the legendary Vladimir Antonov-Ovseyenko, who had led the Bolshevik seizure of power in Petrograd in 1917, had died in Stalin's prisons. Like many grown children of Stalin's leading victims, Anton had himself "sat" in the Gulag for almost thirteen years, an experience that shaped almost everything he did later, from his prosecutorial writings and the risks he took to his several marriages and choice of friends.

Nearly blind, but wiry and determined, Anton was capable of boundless research and writing (as well as an astonishing number of chin-ups, even two decades later, in his eighties). Like another former zek, Solzhenitsyn, he was embattled, willful, and overly confident in his Gulag-acquired cunning. As our friendship developed, his frequent requests for my assistance in exposing "Stalinist hangmen," past and present, sometimes worried me. But Anton, like Roy, was admired and trusted by many Gulag survivors, and he too persuaded them to help me.

My third enabler was Tatyana Bayeva, a remarkable woman in her thirties at the center of Moscow's beleaguered human rights movement. (A famous "Demonstration of Seven on Red Square" protesting the Soviet invasion of Czechoslovakia in August 1968 actually included an eighth person—the twenty-one-year-old Tanya Bayeva. She was arrested, but, unlike the others, not punished, except for being expelled from her academic institute.) The movement's ranks also included survivors of Stalin's terror as well as many children of victims who did not return. Indeed, Tanya's father, Aleksandr Bayev, a much-honored, internationally known biochemist and high official in the Soviet Academy of Sciences in the 1970s, had spent seventeen years in Stalinist camps and exile, where she was born.[12] Living in the same Moscow building, Tanya and I became close friends as the result of a neighborly encounter.

Though overlooked in most accounts, women formed the infrastructure of the Soviet dissident movement from the late 1960s to the mid-1980s. They typed the *samizdat*, organized its distribution, arranged havens for materials and people on the move, and tried to keep the men from drinking too much. Few were more committed or important than Tanya Bayeva. Her small apartment, laden with manuscripts and forbidden books published abroad, was a regular meeting place for human rights activists and other dissidents. Among them were middle-aged survivors of the terror, especially men smitten with Tanya's exotic looks, worldly manner, and aura of a keeper of many secrets. Several of these people also became valuable sources of information for me.

By the early 1980s, due mostly to Anna Larina, Roy, Anton, and Tanya, I had come to know more than twenty Gulag survivors or other terror victims. During periodic stays in Moscow, I interviewed them at various lengths, a few repeatedly, alone or at small private gatherings, but always in strict confidence, as the times required. Each had returned from his or her own Golgotha, a word they often used. Many of their names would be familiar to Russian readers, but not to American ones. Nonetheless, I feel obliged to mention some of them here both to acknowledge their help and to give readers a sense of who they were.

Most of those in middle age when I met them had been arrested or otherwise punished as children of prominent Stalin victims with political ties to Bukharin. Yuri Aikhenvald and Leonid Petrovsky were sons of well-known young Bukharinists of the 1920s. Natalya Rykova's father, Aleksei Rykov, was Lenin's successor as Soviet premier and Bukharin's erstwhile ally in the leadership; the writer Kamil Ikramov's father headed the Soviet Uzbek Communist Party. Both men were tried and executed with Bukharin in 1938. Igor Pyatnitsky's father, Osip, a high-ranking member of the Party's Central Committee, tried to stop Stalin's terror in 1937 and save Bukharin and the others. He was arrested, horribly beaten, and shot. These children of the once-powerful survived, but they, like so many others, lost many years of their lives.

Other victims I knew well had different political backgrounds. Mikhail Baitalsky, an elderly man I met through Roy, was one of only two known surviving members of the Trotskyist opposition of the 1920s. In the 1960s and 1970s, he became, always under pseudonyms, a prolific and admired *samizdat* writer on subjects ranging from his martyred comrades to Soviet alcoholism and anti-Semitism. Yuri Gastyev, on the other hand, a middle-aged survivor whom prison had made alternately mirthful and forlorn—a condition worsened, it seemed, by an unrequited boyish crush on Tanya—was the son of an executed orthodox Communist poet.

Two older Gulag returnees had, I soon learned, saint-like reputations in non-conformist circles. A Red Army officer and loyal Stalinist at the time, Lev Kopelev had been arrested in Germany in 1945 for protesting the rape of local women by Soviet occupying soldiers. Bear-like and kind, with a white Tolstoian beard, he had spent time with Solzhenitsyn in the Gulag and in 1962 helped arrange Soviet publication of the then-unknown author's sensational camp novel, *One Day in the Life of Ivan Denisovich*. (Solzhenitsyn later portrayed Kopelev unfairly as the dogmatic Lev Rubin in *The First Circle*.) Kopelev's own unflinching accounts of his journey from Stalinist to democratic humanist— *To Be Preserved Forever*, *The Education of a True Believer*, and *Ease My Sorrows*—were widely read in Western translations before they could be published in Russia. He continued to advise me after being stripped of Soviet citizenship in 1981, for his outspoken dissent, while in Germany.

My favorite returnee, however, apart from Anna Larina, of course, was the beloved Yevgeny Gnedin, a man already in his late seventies. A ranking official in the Soviet Foreign Ministry in the 1930s, he was one of the few arrested people who never confessed or incriminated others, despite being beaten for months under Beria's personal supervision. Gnedin's small frame, outwardly soft appearance, and smiling face hardly seemed to fit a person who had endured so much while seeing his friends and colleagues destroyed. Nor did any trace of bitterness taint his extraordinary wisdom and compassion.

After returning to Moscow in 1955 from sixteen years in camps and exile, Gnedin befriended many younger victims who were still struggling with their pasts. He helped a distraught Kamil Ikramov, who spent twelve years in the Gulag from age sixteen and whom Gnedin mentored in camp and exile, for example, to understand, "I should live as though my father is watching me." Gnedin's friends gathered frequently, as I did, at his beckoning apartment. One of them, the poet Vladimir Kornilov, wrote:

Times when I am feeling under,
Something ugly on my chest,
I begin to thirst for Gnedin
Like a sinner for Christ.
. . .
With all five fingers of feeling
I fasten onto his tale.
He teaches me serious matters
And I wish never to fail.[13]

Another was Yuri Larin, for whom Gnedin became the
father he never knew, as well as his secret co-translator of my
biography of Bukharin into Russian. (Gnedin had worked at the
newspaper *Izvestia* in the mid-1930s, when Bukharin was editor.)
Published in the United States in 1980 for clandestine circulation
inside the Soviet Union, the translation was credited to "Y. and
Y. Thursday," the day they regularly met to work. When Gnedin
died in Moscow, in 1983, Yuri wrote to me, "You know who we
have lost . . . Without him, my life would have been so much more
difficult. But he was such a good and radiant person, it seems he
didn't really die."

These Stalinist victims were among those who initially made
my project possible. Somewhat later, there were others, four
of special importance. Mikhail Shatrov, Rykov's nephew and
Natalya's cousin, lost thirty relatives to the terror but nonetheless
later managed to become one of the most popular (and censored)
Soviet playwrights. From his own early life wandering from one
precarious refuge to another, and from his subsequent position in
official cultural life, Shatrov knew a lot about my subject. So did,
in a different way, the older and unfailingly affable Lev Razgon,
a longtime zek and writer of children's books. Razgon had special
perspectives both on victims and their victimizers, and some
Russians rank his tales of the Gulag, published in English as *True
Stories*, with those of Solzhenitsyn and Shalamov.

Aleksandr Milchakov's assistance was different. The son of a Young Communist leader of the 1930s, also Aleksandr, who survived the Gulag, Sasha, as I called him, was a journalist on a mission. In the late 1980s, he led the way in discovering when victims had actually died and where they were buried, focusing attention on Moscow's ancient Donskoi Cemetery. One rainy day, he smuggled me, undetected by the drunken caretaker, inside the now notorious crematorium, where corpses had been burned in the late 1930s and their remains dumped into a common grave. Sasha's articles turned Donskoi into a Mecca for victims' relatives long in need of a place to mourn them. (In 1989, as a CBS News consultant, I helped Mike Wallace film the crematorium's exterior for a *60 Minutes* report. We were barred from entering it this time by a now frantically sober custodian.)

Finally, there was Bukharin's historian daughter, Svetlana Gurvich, by his previous wife, Esfir Gurvich. Svetlana welcomed me only belatedly, but I understood why. Born in 1924, twelve years before her half brother Yuri, and arrested in 1949 with her mother, who had once been a prominent Soviet economist, Svetlana had lived her entire life in the ominous familial shadow of a "heinous enemy of the people." Even in the 1970s, alone with her very aged and infirm mother, in a tiny Moscow apartment and with little income, she felt constantly threatened by neo-Stalinist historians at her academic institute. Contact with me, she feared, especially with my book circulating in Moscow, would further endanger her.

But when Svetlana did eventually embrace me, it was with pent-up enthusiasm that lasted until her death in 2003, though also with her chronically skittish nerves. We were now, she declared, "comrades-in-arms" in the struggle to restore her father's historical reputation. (The comradeship included, I should add, a long list of misjudgments she thought I had made in my book about him.) Still more, Svetlana Gurvich's relatives, on her mother's side, were separate from Anna Larina's, though they too had been persecuted by Stalin. Their experiences provided me with additional cases. In particular, the fate of Svetlana and Esfir taught me more about the special tragedy of women alone during and after the terror, and about who had helped them and who had not.

Readers should not think I collected all these survivor stories through clever planning. Several virtually fell into my lap. In 1982, for instance, Solzhenitsyn's first wife, Natalya Reshetovskaya, unexpectedly asked me to take the manuscript of her voluminous memoirs to the United States for safekeeping. It contained unknown stories of returning zeks she had met through her husband. Two years before, I had a chance encounter with Pavel Aksyonov, mayor of Kazan until his arrest in 1937 and the first husband of Eugenia Ginzburg, the great Gulag memoirist mentioned earlier. It happened at a farewell gathering for their son, the famous writer Vasily Aksyonov, who was emigrating to America because of his own nonconformism. The old man wanted to talk about Bukharin, whom he had known, but also answered my questions about his post-Gulag life. Better than anyone else, he explained how the terror destroyed marriages, even those of survivors, as it had his and Ginzburg's.

I was not the first person to engage survivors of Stalin's terror in oral history—or, as they often said, "living history." In many cases, Solzhenitsyn, Medvedev, or Antonov-Ovseyenko had done so earlier for their uncensored books about the Soviet past.[14] Solzhenitsyn, to take an unfortunate instance, visited Anna Larina in her Moscow apartment in the early 1960s to learn about her experiences in camps and exile. She later regretted meeting him because while Solzhenitsyn profusely praised Bukharin in her presence, he denigrated him in *The Gulag Archipelago*. For Roy and Anton, on the other hand, Larina had only the warmest feelings, though we all worried a bit about Anton's occasional escapades.

I was, however, so far as I know, the first foreigner to interview these Gulag survivors. As such, I was always aware that by helping me, they, unlike myself, might again be at considerable risk. I was therefore very cautious, which usually meant surreptitious. In particular, it meant never mentioning an interview to another person without my subject's permission; never discussing my project or a scheduled meeting on the telephone—one former zek would call Larina and ask, "Has the pie baked?," meaning had I arrived; never going directly from one victim to another; and never leaving any related notes, manuscripts, or books in my apartment or hotel room. (The result of the latter precaution was, according to my doctor, two hernia operations.)

But I soon realized that most of the terror victims I knew were selective cases, people linked to the original Soviet Communist elite and who had lived in Moscow before and after the Gulag.[15] To reach beyond them, I prepared an anonymous Russian-language questionnaire—also the first on the subject—that friends, acquaintances, and people unknown to me circulated more widely inside the Soviet Union and among survivors who had emigrated.[16] By the early 1980s, it had yielded, through various channels, twenty or so detailed written replies.

With cases culled from printed and typescript sources, I now had files on nearly sixty individuals. Considering Stalin's millions of victims, it was a small sample. But considering recent Western generalizations about the entire Stalinist era based on many fewer personal materials found in Soviet archives, it was substantial. (Solzhenitsyn said he "collected 227 testimonies" for *The Gulag Archipelago*, but many of them were letters he received from former zeks after the publication of his novel about the camps, *One Day in the Life of Ivan Denisovich*.)[17]

By then, I was running out of time to pursue the project inside the Soviet Union. My Moscow double life—as an official exchange scholar working on an approved subject while increasingly engrossed in a disapproved one—had become known to Soviet authorities, as had my growing role in sending banned memoirs and contemporary dissident materials out of the country and Russian-language books published abroad back into the Soviet Union. My sporadic "tail" became more constant, and a KGB officer, as the secret police was then called, at an institute I occasionally visited bluntly warned me to "stop spending time with people who have grievances against the Soviet government." (Whether he meant Gulag survivors or latter-day dissidents, I didn't ask.)

Indeed, the noose had been tightening around my small Moscow world for several years. In 1979, copies of the American edition of my Bukharin book were seized at the International Moscow Book Fair. Within a year, the Russian-language edition, published in the United States, was being regularly confiscated in KGB searches of private homes, along with books by Solzhenitsyn, Medvedev, Conquest, and Orwell—a compliment perhaps but not a good sign. Also in 1980, the Soviet press unleashed a scurrilous attack on Kopelev, prelude to nullifying his citizenship and Vasily Aksyonov's; Andrei Sakharov, father of the Soviet hydrogen bomb and the leading liberal dissident, whom I knew, was banished from Moscow; and Father Dmitri Dudko, a maverick priest who lived in Roy's building, where a KGB guard noted all visitors, was arrested.

In 1982, two related events directly affected me. In April, the KGB carried out a surprise, five-hour search of Antonov-Ovseyenko's apartment. Still worse, Anna Larina happened to arrive when it was under way, and was forced to remain several hours. During an angry exchange between Anton and the secret police agents, she heard my name mentioned. (Having repeatedly warned me against leaving incriminating materials in my Moscow apartment, the cunning zek had kept our clandestine correspondence in his.) Soon after, in a confidential report to the Kremlin leadership, the head of the KGB, Yuri Andropov, harshly condemned Anton's "illegal and anti-Soviet" activities. He singled out Anton's book, *The Time of Stalin: Portrait of a Tyranny*, published the year before in New York.[18] I had taken the manuscript out of the country, as the KGB by then no doubt knew.

Whether because of my role as a conduit for such materials, my own book, or my returnee project, I was banished from the Soviet Union, unable to obtain an entry visa after mid-1982, despite my repeated requests for one. On several occasions, my application was supported by at least two ranking Soviet officials, including a member of the Communist Party Central Committee, but to no avail. An indelible mark, it seemed, had been put by my name, where it remained for the next three years.

Changes in my personal life may have contributed to this political development. When I began interviewing Gulag survivors, in 1976, I was living in Moscow with my wife, Lynn, and our young children, Andrew and Alexandra, none of whom spoke Russian. Family obligations limited the time I had for my unofficial project and thus made it less conspicuous. By the early 1980s, however, my marriage had dissolved and my traveling companion was Katrina vanden Heuvel, later my wife and now editor and publisher of *The Nation* magazine. With knowledge of Russian and an affinity for political victims due to her work on McCarthyism, she was an enthusiastic participant in my project. We spent most of our Moscow time, while on the same official exchange, in the company of Stalin's victims and dissidents. Not surprisingly, Katrina too was denied a Soviet visa after mid-1982.

My three-year absence from Moscow was filled with concerns about Anna Larina's family and the other Russians who had helped me. But it also gave me more time to write, while still teaching at the university. I had already collected a very large quantity of materials about Stalin's victims, some of which I used in two more general books I published during that period.[19] I also drafted the summary of the large volume I intended to write about Gulag survivors and their return to society.

That intention was overwhelmed after 1985 by the drama of Mikhail Gorbachev's reforms. For me, the new Soviet leader's policies represented the attempted Soviet reformation I had long considered possible, as well as the possibility of previously inaccessible archive documents for a fuller edition of my biography of Bukharin. In 1985, our visa problems solved, Katrina and I began spending as much time as we could in Moscow in order to observe the unfolding of those historic events.

Within two years, the ending of censorship had filled the Soviet press with new details about Stalin's terror. Now less fearful, survivors began to tell their stories publicly and, having heard from friends about my interest, search me out. Though no longer my main purpose, I never stopped collecting information from the dwindling number of Gulag returnees, even after the Soviet Union ended in 1991, the year our daughter, Nika, was born. Katrina and I continued to meet with Stalin's victims, often late into the night while Nika, with only a faint understanding of who they were, slept on their sofas. (Anna Larina died in 1996, when Nika was five, but she remembered the elderly woman she called *bulya*, or "grandma," and years later wrote about her for a college admissions essay.)

But other projects—writing about the rise and fall of Gorbachev's reformation and discovering archive materials about Bukharin—were now my priority. My swollen returnee files languished in overflowing cabinets and cartons in my New York apartment and Princeton office until the mid-1990s, when I met a young American scholar, Nanci Adler. Impressed by her very similar project, and by her grasp of psychological and comparative approaches I lacked, I gave her full access to everything I had collected for her own excellent book, which appeared in 2002.[20] At the time, I probably thought it was a form of closure.

Why, then, publish this book now, more than thirty years after I began it? The most compelling reason is that I never actually lost the uneasy feeling of having left work unfinished and obligations unfulfilled, even though fewer and fewer of the victims I knew were still alive. I was waiting, it seems, for an impetus to finish what I had abandoned. It came in 2007, bringing the history of the project full-circle, when Bob Conquest's friends decided to prepare a volume of essays on the occasion of his ninetieth birthday. I contributed a revised version of the summary I had drafted in 1983. Working on it rekindled my enthusiasm and led to this book.

Another reason to publish *The Victims Return* now is to counter the impression, widespread in the West, that knowledge about such Soviet-era subjects was impossible before Gorbachev ended censorship or even before the post-Soviet "archive revolution." In fact, as we know also from other historical atrocities, crimes like Stalin's leave behind survivors who will bear witness even in the face of state repression. As the Russian historian Vladlen Loginov recently wrote, "Every era gives rise to its own specific types of sources,"[21] including the kinds in this book.

Most importantly, Gulag returnees remain a little-known subject, certainly compared to survivors of the Jewish Holocaust. As an American author recently noted, their saga is "often ignored" even in histories of the Soviet Union.[22] Khrushchev-era returnees sometimes appear in Russian and Western fiction, such as Vasily Grossman's *Everything Flows*, Vasily Aksyonov's *The Burn*, Andrei Bitov's *Pushkin House*, Martin Amis' *House of Meetings*, and Tom Rob Bell's recent novels. A few memoirs of post-Gulag lives have been published in Russia, notably ones by Kopelev and by Yevfrosiniya Kersnovskaya, which contain her remarkable drawings of what she experienced. And testimonies of Stalin's victims have informed more general Western studies.[23] But despite many available materials, Adler's study remains the only real examination of this "great return," inexplicably even in Russia itself.[24] The story, as two former zeks wrote to me from Israel in 2009, is "a still-unfinished chronicle."

My book is not the large volume I originally planned, but it can serve, I hope, as an overview of the political and social dimensions of the Gulag returnee phenomenon. In addition, my perspectives are somewhat different from those of other writers, possibly because my initial research was done in closer proximity to the actual events, when many victims (and victimizers) were still alive. Having known so many of them personally has no doubt influenced what I have written here, for better or worse.

The themes and subjects of this book are the ones I drafted in 1983, but significantly expanded with information that has since become available. (My endnotes cite related publications since 1983, some of which I read in typescript before they could be published.) More recent materials have enabled me to develop various matters that I knew less well three decades ago. And though the primary focus of the book is still on the Khrushchev years, I have added an account of the saga of terror victims from his fall from official favor, and theirs, in 1964 to the present.

Even now, however, I have not divulged the names of all the people who, trusting in my pledge of confidentiality, helped me in the 1970s and 1980s. Even though most of them are now dead, I remain reticent about several identities for the sake of their surviving relatives, partly because of uncertain developments in Russia today—or perhaps simply because of promises I made and habits I adopted long ago.

CHAPTER 2

Liberation

Most likely I will be rehabilitated posthumously.

—Lev Gumilyov, 1955

Everything has to be done urgently. Otherwise the people will die, they will perish. If everything drags on for years, they will not survive.

—Olga Shatunovskaya, 1956

Stalin's despotic power and mass terror were defining elements of the Soviet political system for almost twenty-five years. When he finally died, on March 5, 1953, some change for the better was therefore certain, though most of his surviving victims did not immediately understand the new situation. Like the rest of the nation, they were stunned by Stalin's death. Having lived so long with the omnipresent cult of a god-like leader, they could not imagine life without him. Many victims, Anna Larina and Lev Kopelev later recalled, feared the result would be even worse: only Stalin, they reasoned, knew they were actually innocent, and his fearful successors would now execute all the surviving "enemies of the people."

But other prisoners understood that a historic change was already under way. Stalin's funeral music filled Lev Razgon with "a sense of incipient liberty," though two more years would pass before he was freed. For Kamil Ikramov, the announcement of Stalin's death "was the first time I felt happy" because "he died and I still had not." Still earlier, when official bulletins reported that Stalin was suffering from "Cheyne-Stokes respiration," Yuri Gastyev knew it was a pre-death syndrome and immediately hailed the British doctors Cheyne and Stokes, who had discovered the breathing pattern, as "great benefactors of mankind."[1] (Years later, when published criticism of Stalin was again forbidden, Gastyev made a habit of citing the two "great doctors" in his censored books and articles, to the amusement of knowing friends.)

The zeks who soon began to return were survivors in almost the full sense of survivors of the Nazi extermination camps. (Even Soviet publications later charged Stalin with "genocide against his own people," indeed the "cruelest" in "the history of . . . the entire civilized world.")[2] Unlike Hitler's camps, the Gulag's primary purpose was forced labor; but, as we saw, Stalin's prisons and camps also killed many millions of people. Most of those liberated in the 1950s had been arrested in the 1940s or later, surviving "only" ten years or less.

Survival was therefore a subject that troubled Gulag returnees, much as it had tormented Nazi camp victims. Who had survived, and why? Many attributed it to "pure chance" or a "miracle,"[3] but there were also specific reasons. Some people endured because of strong bodies and unrelenting wills, the good fortune of less arduous work, or early release into exile. Others did so by becoming informers, providing sexual favors, or collaborating in different ways with camp authorities. Returnees I knew usually did not want to discuss the issue or did so without recriminations, but several accused other survivors of perfidious behavior. Unfairly, I thought, accusations were often directed at women. About an actress who regained her prominence after the Gulag, for example, it was rumored, "Even in the camps she managed to bill and coo."[4] Cruder epithets trailed another former beauty: "She fucked her way through the camps."

Such moments made me uncomfortable, as when a survivor showed me a disfigured family photo album from the 1930s. In a desperate but futile attempt to save herself, the wife of an arrested top official had crudely excised every image of her husband, leaving only a hand, arm, or shoulder touching prominent figures still in political favor. (It was a frequent act of panic during the terror years.)[5] The person who showed me the album added, "And that's how she behaved in the camp," expecting me to share her indignation. I always declined making such judgments, explaining that never having faced those kinds of life-and-death choices, I could not be sure how I would have behaved.

Because of the scope and duration of Stalin's terror, we still do not know exactly how many victims survived to be freed after his death. According to internal Gulag reports, 5.5 million souls were still in camps, labor colonies, prisons, and exile settlements.[6] The actual number was almost certainly larger. Camp commandants, who prepared the reports, frequently understated the number of their forced laborers in order to meet production levels demanded by Moscow based on that number. In addition, the reports probably do not include all the prisons throughout the vast Soviet Union. Nor do they appear to include the large number of zeks who, having served their camp time, were sent individually into "eternal exile" in remote small towns and villages or people, like Bukharin's daughter, sentenced only to exile.

Whatever the total number of political victims in captivity in 1953, to them must be added the uncounted millions of relatives of "enemies of the people"—or in another formulation of Stalinist repression, "wives and children of traitors to the Motherland." (Some citizens renounced their accused kin or managed to hide such relationships, but many others would not or could not.) The story of all those collateral victims—relatives whose spouses, parents, or siblings became the inadvertent "culprit" of their misfortune, as the poet Anna Akhmatova's son, Lev Gumilyov, characterized her involuntary role in his arrest[7]—remains largely unwritten.

The fate of children who had been "careless in choosing their parents," another bitter remark attributed to Gumilyov, was especially tragic. As a result of the terror, orphaned children and their "destroyed childhoods"—a few even killed themselves—became a "commonplace story."[8] Early in Stalin's mass repressions, he issued a particularly cynical declaration: "The son is not responsible for the father." In reality, the NKVD had orders "to take" most of the children as well. Older ones, like those I knew and mentioned earlier, were usually sent to the Gulag, but so were many young ones. According to one source, 4 to 5 million children passed through special NKVD-run or Gulag facilities over the years, though not all of them orphaned by the terror.[9]

In some instances, very young children were saved from those institutions by determined relatives who literally snatched them from orphanages or from the NKVD itself. This was the comparative good fortune of Maya Plisetskaya, the later internationally renowned ballerina; the playwright Shatrov; Vasily Aksyonov, whose novels and short stories had a Vonnegut-like following among Soviet youth in the 1960s; and an eventual Russian ambassador to the United States, Vladimir Lukin. (I knew Lukin in the late 1970s, through his friend Tanya Bayeva, when his academic career had barely recovered from his nonconformist political views.)

But sooner or later, many children ended up in NKVD-approved orphanages. (A few secret police officers and camp guards took infants for themselves, adopting them.) Most grew up without knowing the fate of their parents, or even who they were, as happened to Yuri Larin, the son of Bukharin and Anna Larina, and already stigmatized in classified files by their parents' arrest. Some orphanages were "relatively happy places," as was Yuri's—he always denied that his years there were "tragic"—with personnel dedicated to their wards' education and well-being.[10] But most were harsh, uncaring, even cruel institutions without adequate facilities, nutrition, or health care. Though it may have been an extreme case, during a two-month period in 1934, sixty children died from "emaciation" in a single provincial orphanage.[11]

Apart from young children, millions of relatives of people "taken" during Stalin's terror remained nominally free but so stigmatized by their "spoiled biographies" they were prohibited from living or working as they desired. The personal questionnaire (*anketa*) in almost every realm of Soviet life, from education and employment to residence and travel, pointedly asked about an applicant's immediate family members. The prohibitions it generated were ubiquitous. Typically, the destitute widow of the young Bukharinist Pyotr Petrovsky, Leonid's mother and father, was unable to obtain essential social benefits for herself and her younger child.[12]

And yet, because the terror and its impresario were capricious, there were notable exceptions—people who achieved officially honored careers under Stalin despite the arrest and even execution of close relatives. At the top of the list were members of Stalin's own leadership council, the Politburo, including his oldest and closest associate, Vyacheslav Molotov, and the country's nominal president, Mikhail Kalinin. The despot had their wives arrested and sent to the Gulag, while the divorced-by-repression husbands retained their positions at the apex of the political system.

Other members of victimized families were equally well known to most Russians, though not their dark political secret. Plisetskaya, whose father was shot in 1938, began her long career at the Bolshoi Theater in 1943. The famous stage and film actress

Olga Aroseva, whose executed father had been a prominent Communist official, was an analogous case. So was the best-known and most favored Soviet political caricaturist, Boris Yefimov, whose brother, the journalist Mikhail Koltsov, had been shot. In a very different profession, Mikhail Kalashnikov designed the Soviet Army's legendary AK-47 weapon even though his father had died in exile and his brother was in the Gulag. And while Igor Netto became a national soccer star, his brother Lev sat in a camp.

I know little about how those celebrated public figures coped with their personal ordeals. Plisetskaya and Aroseva stayed as far from politics as they could, even while performing in Stalin's presence, Yefimov, who lived nearly seventy years longer than his brother, dying in 2008 at the age of one hundred and nine, later wrote detailed accounts of trying to save his sibling. Documents confirm that Yefimov made queries, but people who knew him doubted he ever took any risks on behalf of his brother, pointing to his vicious drawings of Stalin's leading victims. As for Netto, it is said he only worried that his brother's arrest would spoil his athletic career.[13] Here too I cannot judge.

Each of these personal dramas had the makings of a profound Russian novel, but two seemed especially anguished. One was that of Sergei Vavilov, the younger brother of the internationally acclaimed geneticist Nikolai Vavilov and himself a prominent scientist. Nikolai disappeared in 1940, wasting away in prison cells until he died from physical abuse and neglect in 1943. For Sergei, "the horror hanging over my brother" was "unbearable torture." By all accounts, he did everything he could, at considerable personal risk, to save his brother and help his family. When Sergei learned privately of Nikolai's death, he wrote in his diary, "My own soul is frozen and becomes a stone. I work and live as a robot."[14]

Nonetheless, in 1945, Stalin, to deflect Western concerns about Nikolai Vavilov, suddenly appointed Sergei Vavilov president of the Soviet Academy of Sciences, a highly prestigious position.

Some of Sergei's colleagues were shocked that he accepted the position, but he used it to appeal repeatedly to Stalin for Nikolai's exoneration, once even threatening to resign. In January 1951, evidently overcome by pent-up torment, Sergei traveled secretly to a prison in Saratov, where his brother had died, in search of eyewitnesses and his grave, to no avail. A few days after returning to Moscow, Sergei Vavilov suddenly died, almost to the day of his brother's death. He was buried with state honors.

The other case was somewhat different but no less tragic. The brothers Dmitri and Grigory Maretsky were reviled young Bukharin followers executed in the late 1930s, but their sister, Vera Maretskaya, became the country's most beloved actress and recipient of four Stalin prizes.[15] Maretskaya kept her family tragedy secret, not even telling a co-worker who had been in the Gulag. But she used her stature privately to have her younger sister freed from the Gulag after two years, in 1943, and soon after Stalin's death her brothers posthumously exonerated, almost without precedent at the time. (Because of her Bukharinist brothers, when Maretskaya learned in the 1960s from Anna Larina's other son, Mikhail, that his mother had survived, the famous actress immediately reached out to her.)

We may wonder how Maretskaya, a lonely woman who died of brain cancer in 1978 without any immediate family, bore her tragedy while performing so publicly and being honored by the man who had ordered her brothers' execution. She endured, it is said, through her inner strength, lifelong love of acting, and enormous talent. Assigned stereotypical Stalinist roles, she infused them with her art and personal sorrow, transforming several into iconic Soviet characters. Eventually, they made her untouchable, if there was any such person under Stalin.

But eminent careers in families victimized by the terror were, I should reemphasize, exceptions. The great majority of relatives of condemned "counterrevolutionaries" suffered such deprivations that decades later, in the 1990s, the Russian government finally acknowledged formally they too had been "repressed," especially the children whose lives had been "no less tragic than the fate of their repressed parents."[16] Like survivors of the Gulag, they also wanted full exoneration and integration into Soviet society.

We are left, then, with only an approximate estimate of the number of political victims of Stalin's terror still alive when he died in 1953. Considering all the people in various kinds of captivity and their immediate family members, there must have been at least 15 million, and probably more. Indeed, it was frequently said that "every family, in both the countryside and the cities," suffered during the twenty-four-year terror.[17]

—⟋ⱶⱶⱶ⟍—

Many people had been released through the Gulag's "revolving door" over the years,[18] most of them sentenced as ordinary criminals, not political offenders, and many already dying. But the post-Stalin liberation was entirely different—profoundly political, fraught with questions of innocence and culpability, and the source of fearful conflicts in the Kremlin.

In March 1953, soon after Stalin died, a government amnesty released 1 million camp inmates, mainly criminals serving short terms. Much has been made in Western writing about the Gulag, as it was in the Soviet Union, about the difference between political and non-political convictions. In practice, given the draconian nature of Stalinist law, the distinction was often blurred and sometimes non-existent. Sentencing starving peasants to the Gulag for taking bits of "collective" food, or factory workers for being late, would be considered political repression in most societies. Whatever the actual differences in the Gulag in 1953, the freeing of prisoners classified as "politicals" unfolded slowly over the next three years, agonizingly for those still there.[19]

The primary reason was, of course, the post-Stalin leadership's complicity in his crimes. All of its leading members had blood on their hands—Beria, Molotov, Lazar Kaganovich, Kliment Voroshilov, Georgy Malenkov, Anastas Mikoyan, and Nikita Khrushchev himself. And there were plenty of secret documents and surviving witnesses to testify to the role they had played in the terror. Among those longtime Party and state bosses there were, however, significantly different degrees of personal responsibility and thus vulnerability.

The older members of the new leadership, who had been closest to Stalin, were the most complicit. Beria had headed the terror apparatus for many years, personally torturing victims, and, as a sideline, was known to be a serial rapist of women and girls, sometimes threatening to arrest or promising to free their relatives. Molotov and Kaganovich had co-signed with Stalin more lists condemning people than anyone else. Voroshilov had carried out the massacre of tens of thousands of Soviet military officers on the eve of World War II. And Malenkov, though younger, had supervised one of Stalin's last mass repressions in Leningrad. The complicity of Mikoyan and Khrushchev had been on a lesser scale and farther from the center. Only they, it turned out, demonstrated remorse and acted on it.

During the three years following Stalin's death, the plight of his surviving victims loomed ever larger in the struggle for power among his successors. Again, only Khrushchev, who gradually emerged as the top but not unchallengeable leader, and Mikoyan gave any signs of being willing to reopen the entire question of Stalin's victims. (Before his arrest in 1953, Beria also did so, apparently in an attempt to diminish his vulnerability.) Stalin's other heirs resisted, thwarted initiatives, and tried to minimize the extent of the crimes and cover up their role in them. So did Khrushchev's own compromised appointee as head of the KGB, the NKVD's successor organization, Ivan Serov.[20] As late as 1957, Molotov, Kaganovich, and their allies had thwarted Khrushchev's effort to exonerate Kamil Ikramov's father, for example, for more than a year.

As happens when power-holders are unwilling or unable to act decisively, the new leadership resorted to ponderous bureaucratic procedures to review the status of political prisoners. Even though millions had been convicted by extra-legal troikas, only the Military Tribunal of the Supreme Court and the Procurator-General—the counterpart of the U.S. Attorney General but with greater discretionary powers—could overturn convictions of Article 58 "counterrevolutionaries." Both were swamped by appeals from surviving victims and from relatives of those who had perished. And while Khrushchev's new Procurator-General, Roman Rudenko, seemed open to rectifying injustices, many lower-ranking procurators implicated in old cases were not.[21]

Apart from surviving Jewish doctors arrested in Stalin's final terror scenario, who were freed soon after his death, the result was more bureaucratic obstacles and paperwork than releases from prisons, camps, or exile. One case reopened as late as 1955 generated a file larger than the one on which the victim had been sentenced. Most of the returnees I knew had their initial appeals flatly rejected, some more than once. Appealing to the Procuracy in 1954, Kopelev, like many others, was informed he "had no basis for a review" because he had been "sentenced correctly."[22] He remained in the Gulag two more years.

Political prisoners with the best chance of early release were several hundred personally known to the current Party leaders or to other influential figures. The beneficiaries included Molotov's wife; a few once-prominent Communist officials such as Milchakov (Sasha's father), Olga Shatunovskaya, and Aleksei Snegov, the latter two having been close to Khrushchev and Mikoyan before their arrest in the 1930s and who were to play important roles later in the 1950s; and several grown children of executed officials Khrushchev had also known. The latter group included my friend Igor Pyatnitsky and Pyotr Yakir, son of a general shot in 1937, who had been in the Gulag since he was fourteen. (The ordeal made Pyotr a leading and ultimately ill-fated figure in the Soviet dissident movement of the 1960s and 1970s.)[23]

A remarkable number of once-famous performers were also released early. Most had survived by providing entertainment for camp authorities. Among them were the actresses Tatyana Okunevskaya, who had been raped by Beria prior to her arrest and whose last film was shown in a camp with her name deleted from the credits, and Zoya Fyodorova, whose daughter Victoria's relations with her American father and her American husband inspired a book that still tempts movie producers; Eddi Rozner, the most popular Soviet jazzman, called "the white Louis Armstrong" by Satchmo himself, until Stalin banned his music in 1946; the four Starostin brothers, soccer stars and coaches of the legendary Spartak team; and the filmmaker Aleksei Kapler, arrested for having an affair with Stalin's sixteen-year-old daughter, Svetlana. (The initial affair with the forty-year-old Kapler was said to have been "passionate" but non-sexual and consummated only after his release ten years later.)[24]

Compared to the arduous journey home of millions of other victims two or three years later, several of these privileged few were given five-star releases. Instead of a long, uncushioned train ride, Milchakov was flown from Magadan to Moscow. Okunevskaya was given flowers and driven home from her Moscow cell by a KGB major. But Molotov's wife, Polina Zhemchuzhina, may have been the first and most favored returnee. She was freed from a Moscow prison the day after Stalin's funeral, on March 10, 1953, Molotov's birthday. He took her directly to her former home, a Politburo member's luxury apartment, where they resumed their marriage as though it had never been interrupted by her five years in the Gulag.[25]

Otherwise, however, apart from partial amnesties, release procedures were a slow, case-by-case process usually stretching over months, even years, and ending in rejection. Of 237,412 appeals formally reviewed by April 1955, barely 4 percent resulted in release.[26] Spurred in part by rebellions in the camps, large crowds of petitioners assembled outside the Procurator's building in central Moscow, and a mounting flood of appeals sent to the Party's headquarters and to the KGB, the exodus from the Gulag grew. By the end of 1955, 195,353 people had been released, though only 88,278 from forced labor camps and colonies, the rest from various kinds of exile.[27] It was a substantial number, but growing at a pace too slow to save the lives of many left behind. As Gumilyov, eventually an acclaimed ethnographer and Russian nationalist philosopher, wrote despairingly from his camp in 1955, "Most likely I'll be rehabilitated posthumously."[28]

Khrushchev's historic assault on Stalin's still cult-like reputation at a closed session of the Twentieth Party Congress in February 1956, before more than 1400 delegates, was the turning point. The new leader did not tell the full truth about the terror, or even mention the Gulag, but by accusing the dead tyrant of "mass repressions" over many years, Khrushchev tacitly exonerated millions of falsely condemned victims. Viewed in retrospect, his courageous, frequently explicit revelations before a still largely Stalinist assembly of the Communist Party elite made possible, albeit twenty years later, Mikhail Gorbachev's more far-reaching anti-Stalinism. Certainly that is the belief of the many Russians who even today blame Khrushchev for having mortally undermined the Soviet system.

His nearly four-hour speech remained unpublished in the Soviet Union for thirty years, but it was never "secret," as is usually said. Nor did Khrushchev intend it to be. He ordered the text read at Communist and Young Communist meetings across the country—everywhere from educational, cultural, and military institutions to city and rural workplaces. Formally, it meant that within a few months the Party's 25 million full and apprentice members had heard Khrushchev's revelations about Stalin's terror, including searing details of brutal torture and summary executions. But many more Soviet citizens also heard about them because most of the normally closed meetings were declared "open," and people who attended told others.[29]

The three-year policy of case-by-case, selective releases of surviving victims was no longer tenable, as was also Khrushchev's intent. Even before the 1956 Party congress, he had gathered around him a group of recently freed Communist veterans, notably Shatunovskaya and Snegov. Both implored Khrushchev and Mikoyan to "urgently" liberate all the political prisoners in camps and exile: "Otherwise . . . they will not survive." At Shatunovskaya's urging, Khrushchev issued a decree designed to "simply free immediately" all those in exile without any legal or bureaucratic procedures.[30] His February speech initiated a parallel process of mass liberation of the camps using accelerated formal and improvised means.

The most decisive was the formation in Moscow, also at the suggestion of Shatunovskaya and Snegov, of ninety-seven commissions to be sent directly to the Gulag's sixty-five or so largest camps. Each commission was supposed to have three to seven members, including Party and state officials, and, to insure "objectivity and justice," one already freed and exonerated veteran Communist, though the latter was often excluded. All the commissions were empowered to review cases on the scene and release prisoners. Some, staffed by unsympathetic Party, Procuracy, or KGB officials, did not act justly, but many did so. (The chairman of one commission, the future Party boss of Soviet Ukraine Pyotr Shelest, said what he saw and learned stayed with him the rest of his life.)[31]

This dramatic episode of Soviet traveling committees of liberation, or "unloading parties" as zeks called them, awaits its historian. Several first-hand accounts relate the waves of personal emotions that followed the commissions through the Gulag. One of the fullest appears in the memoirs of the legendary Russian expert on Siberian gold-mining, Vadim Tumanov, then a forced-labor zek in Kolyma. By 1956, he had been in camps for eight years. Rumors of the commissions had already reached distant Kolyma, but when one finally arrived in July, Tumanov and his fellow victims expected only more bureaucratic deceit.

Instead, the thirteen camp officials and commission members around the table, some in KGB or Procuracy uniforms, greeted Tumanov "cheerfully" and solemnly reviewed his case. Other cases had taken only a few minutes, but the commission needed two and a half hours to examine Tumanov's thick files and hear supporting comments by camp authorities and his declaration of innocence. The chairman then rose and announced: "The commission, authorized by the Presidium of the Supreme Soviet of the USSR to re-examine prisoners' cases, frees you and overturns your conviction in the firm belief you will enter the ranks of people building a bright future." Unable to speak, the rugged Tumanov's "eyes filled with tears." He thought to request, however, that the panel also release his fellow miners.[32]

Similar dramas were being enacted throughout the far-flung Gulag. Within a few months, according to official reports, the traveling commissions freed some 100,000 zeks, though other sources give a considerably larger figure. Whatever the exact number, it added significantly to the ever-growing mass exodus from the Gulag. By 1959, most of Stalin's surviving political victims had been released.[33] Among those liberated by the commissions were several of the returnees I knew twenty years later, as well as Akhmatov's embittered son, Lev Gumilyov. So was Lev Netto, who made his way home at the same time his brother Igor was captaining the Soviet soccer team to Olympic Gold in Melbourne.

In the aftermath of Khrushchev's February 1956 speech, the homeward trek of Stalin's victims became a familiar sight on trains and streets across the Soviet Union. With nothing more than documents authorizing their release and destination, a railway ticket, and a few rubles for food, many looked emaciated and aged. Those returning directly from camps, without a term in the harsh but relatively recuperative conditions of exile, had the appearance of "shattered people." One described himself as merely "bones in my body and skin stretched over them." Seeing themselves for the first time in a train mirror, their "faces eaten away by the cold of Siberia and foul air of overcrowded camp barracks," was often a shock.

Arriving at railway stations throughout the country, many returnees clutched a battered suitcase they had lugged through their years in the Gulag like a trophy of survival. (Anna Larina kept hers in a closet until she died, displaying it occasionally to illustrate an episode in her past. Her only other Gulag relic was a hand-made gruel spoon, a birthday gift from another zek.) Bystanders later recalled that many returnees, with shaved heads, were still wearing labor-camp padded jackets and tattered boots. When one released zek visited Communist Party headquarters embarrassed by how he was dressed, a former prisoner now working there, Olga Shatunovskaya, assured him, "It's nothing. Many people are walking around Moscow today in such clothes."[34]

Not all released inmates and exiles actually went home. Some arrested in connection with sensitive political cases, like Bukharin's previous wife, their daughter Svetlana, and his younger brother Vladimir, were issued restrictive documents banning them from Moscow and other large cities for several years. A few, like Kopelev, tried to settle illegally in Moscow but were quickly evicted by the militia. They had to begin rebuilding their lives in provincial towns where opportunities were even fewer. Nor were all deported nationalities permitted to return to their Soviet homelands. One reason was the government's fear that houses and other property long since taken by other citizens would provoke serious conflicts, as indeed they did in years to come.

For many other freed victims, home no longer existed. The poet (and former zek) Nikolai Zabolotsky recalled them "in a field somewhere near Magadan," old men "used up, all passion spent," having "turned their faces from the ways of men." Years of imprisonment had deprived them of their families, careers, possessions, and sense of belonging. Some even preferred the routines of the Gulag, where conditions had improved somewhat since 1953, to the uncertainties of freedom. As Vasily Grossman recalled in his novel *Everything Flows*:

> He had met such old men more than once. They had lost all desire to leave the camp. It was their home. They were fed at regular hours. Kind comrades sometimes gave them little scraps. There was the warmth of the stove.

But, Grossman added, for most of them there was "no higher happiness than to leave the camp . . . and die—even only ten yards from that accursed barbed wire."[35]

For other compelling reasons, hundreds of thousands of former prisoners remained in the vast regions of the diminished Gulag empire, especially in Siberia and Central Asia. (According to Solzhenitsyn, they were the "sensible" ones,[36] though his own literary ambitions propelled him toward Moscow.) They stayed because of new families, salaries offered by state enterprises desperate for their now voluntary labor, and psychological attachments to the primitive expanses of their captivity. Tumanov remained in Siberia in order to pioneer innovative gold-extraction enterprises. Pavel Negretov, whose evocative memoirs, *All Roads Lead to Vorkuta*, were sent to the West by Roy Medvedev and me, became a professional geologist in that city, obtaining a higher degree by correspondence from Leningrad University.[37]

For a few decades, the presence of so many freed victims transformed former Gulag capitals like Magadan, Vorkuta, and Norilsk for the better. But long after the Gulag's barbed wire and watch towers had been bulldozed, visitors continued to come across terrible traces of that world—crumbling barracks, mass graves, skulls with bullet holes. They also found living remnants—elderly survivors and a large number of their descendents. Most would fall on new hard times, former zeks and camp guards alike, when the post-Soviet state ended essential subsidies to those remote regions.[38]

But millions of survivors did go home in the 1950s, or tried to. They were people once as diverse as the Soviet Union itself, formerly of all classes, professions, and nationalities. Over the decades, Stalin's terror had victimized virtually every social group, high and low. In the Gulag, however, as the anti-Stalinist poet and editor Aleksandr Tvardovsky, whose own peasant parents had been deported, wrote:

> ... Fate made everyone equal
> Outside the limits of the law,
> Son of a kulak or Red commander,
> Son of a priest or commissar.
>
> Here classes all were equalized,
> All men were brothers, campmates all,
> Branded as traitors everyone.[39]

Now, burdened by a common past, they went their separate ways.

КАРТА ГУЛАГА

"Map of the Gulag" with dots marking the centers of the main clusters of camps from the 1930s to the 1950s. (Courtesy of Memorial)

Train to the Gulag from the series "Requiem." (Courtesy of the artist, Aleksandr Lozenko)

A defaced photo of Akmal Ikramov, Kamil's father, after his arrest; and 1939 prison photo of the director Vsevolod Meyerhold before being tortured. (From David King's books *The Commissar Vanishes* and *Ordinary Citizens*)

Depictions by the artist Igor Obrosov of "interrogations" in Stalinist prisons based on the memories of his brother. (Courtesy of the State Museum of the History of The Gulag, Moscow)

Above, an NKVD execution squad in 1936. (From David King, *Ordinary Citizens*) Below, a rear entry and the interior of the crematorium at Moscow's Donskoi Cemetery.

From the illustrated memoirs of Yevfrosiniya Kersnovskaya. Above, separating men and women prisoners upon their arrival at the camp. Below, "hard, thankless labor." (Courtesy of Igor Chapkovsky)

From top to bottom, remnants of a camp; punishment cell; and a camp cemetery. (Courtesy of Memorial)

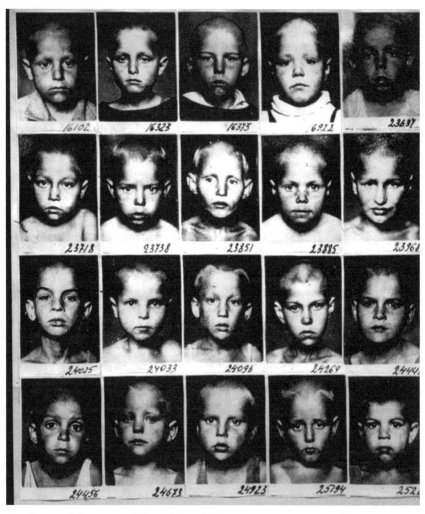

Orphans of the terror. (From David King, *Ordinary Citizens*)

Top left, Nikolai Bukharin (on the right) with Stalin atop the Lenin Mausoleum, 1929. Top right, Nikita Khrushchev (front row in white blouse) seated between the new NKVD chief, Lavrenti Beria, and Stalin, 1938. Bottom, Khrushchev (front row center) at the height of the terror with the then head of the NKVD, Nikolai Yezhov (seated left), and Anastas Mikoyan (standing far left), 1937.

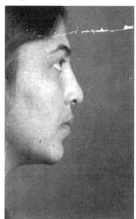

Top left, Anna Larina, 1931; and top right, in prison, 1937. Bottom left, her son Yuri in his orphanage, about 1949. Bottom right, Anna and Yuri's first meeting in her place of Siberian exile, with her other children, Nadya and Misha, 1956.

Left, Esfir and Svetlana Gurvich-Bukharin, about 1929. Below, Svetlana's prison photo, 1949. Bottom: left, Esfir in a Gulag camp, 1955; and right, with Svetlana in Moscow, 1968. (The 1929 and 1955 photos courtesy of Emma Gurvich)

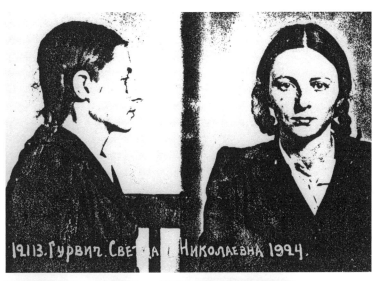

12113. Гурвич Светлана Николаевна 1994.

Vladimir Bukharin, Nikolai's brother, in 1927 and after the Gulag, 1955. (Courtesy of his family)

Natalya Rykova in 1936 and after many years in the Gulag. (Courtesy of Mikhail Shatrov)

Above, Yevgeny Gnedin in the mid-1930s and, with his wife Nadezhda and her mother, after release from exile, mid-1950s.

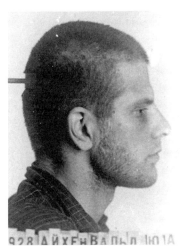

Yuri Aikhenvald's prison photo, 1949; and in Moscow, 1960. (Courtesy of Alexandra Aikhenvald)

Above, Aleksandr Solzhenitsyn posing in his zek camp garb after release from exile, and teaching in a Russian village school, 1957. Below, while still in exile in Kazakhstan, 1955. (Courtesy of Natalya Reshetovskaya)

Olga Shatunovskaya before arrest, 1936; and in a Magadan camp, 1945.

Shatunovskaya (front row, second from the left) with other returnees, including Aleksei Snegov (back row, right), Moscow 1956. (All courtesy of Shatunovskaya family archive)

"Aleksandr Istomin's Crown of Thorns," which could also mean "barbed wire," by the artist Igor Soldatenkov. (Courtesy of Aleksei Soldatenkov)

CHAPTER 3

The Victims Return

*Now those who were arrested will return, and two Russias
will be eyeball to eyeball: The one that put people in the camps
and the one put there.*

—Anna Akhmatova

Many generalizations have been made about survivors of
Stalin's terror—about their health, psychology, families, and
politics—but few of them, if any, are valid. Lives after the Gulag
were almost as diverse as the human condition itself.

Some victims were so broken by their experiences they died
within a few weeks or months of their release—"from freedom,"
it was said.[1] Some died on the way home, on a train, in a railway
station, in a street. A few dropped dead in the camps just after
being notified of their impending release but before the day they
were scheduled to be freed. Such was the case of a middle-aged
man who had survived fifteen years in Kolyma in the hope of once
again seeing his aged mother. She outlived him. For these victims
who survived Stalin, there was no post-Gulag life, no return.

But others achieved astonishingly long lives, especially
considering what they had endured and that male longevity in
Russia even today is less than sixty years. Anna Larina and

Yevgeny Gnedin lived to their early eighties, Bukharin's brother, Vladimir, to eighty-eight. Solzhenitsyn died in 2008, in Moscow, at eighty-nine. Still others lived into their nineties, among them Shatunovskaya, Snegov, Natalya Rykova, who died at ninety-three in 2010, and the well-known film and television actor Georgy Zhzhenov. My friend Anton Antonov-Ovseyenko and the philosopher Grigory Pomerants, Shatunovskaya's confidant after she was ousted from Party headquarters, were still active in Moscow, at ninety, in 2010.

I know of no general explanation for their remarkable longevity. It may be that the people I knew or studied just happened to have extraordinary genes. Or the explanation may be Darwinian: having survived the Gulag, the rest was easy. Or perhaps they were like Lev Gumilyov, who resolved, "The years in camp don't count; it's as though I didn't live them," and was determined to make up for lost time after the Gulag.[2]

The psychology of post-Gulag lives also differed markedly. Some returnees had been so traumatized they remained forever fearful, concealing their past, refusing to discuss it even with family members, and shunning fellow survivors. They became submissive Soviet citizens, "their fear of their own thoughts, their dread of being rearrested, were so overwhelming that they seemed more truly and thoroughly imprisoned than when they had been doing forced labor." Even two of the Gulag's greatest memoirists never fully escaped its legacy. Fearing the manuscript would be discovered, Eugenia Ginzburg burned a "much sharper" draft of her famous book; and Varlam Shalamov, while writing the most unsparing accounts in his *Kolyma Tales*, seemed "frozen by his experience . . . like a blackened tree struck by lightning, which will never again become green."[3]

And yet, other returnees remained "professional zeks," wearing their camp experience like a badge of honor, maintaining lifelong friendships with Gulag comrades, and speaking out because "they could not do otherwise." It took little for Gumilyov to strike "his legendary zek pose" and retell the story of "my Golgotha." Snegov, a Communist truth-teller, replied in character when a hostile Party official asked if he was in the Soviet or anti-Soviet camp, "I am from Kolyma!" Anton's years in the Gulag never ceased being the defining aspect of his defiant identity. And a poet adopted the pen name, "Vladimir Zeka." For them, as for Solzhenitsyn, "the question of whether to conceal his past or be proud of it never arose." (Already a famous Soviet author when summoned by the KGB in 1974, he showed up in his old Gulag clothing. Told that "the masquerade isn't necessary," he was dressed in a new suit and deported to West Germany.)[4]

Many other returnees were neither chronically fearful nor resolutely bold. This was particularly true of ones still young enough to have professional aspirations or ones worried about further stigmatizing their children. Tanya's distinguished father, Aleksandr Bayev, was such a person. After his return in the 1950s, he rose to the top of the Soviet Academy of Sciences without any outward expressions of his seventeen years in the Gulag, confiding only in close friends and trusted colleagues. A decent and tolerant man, he strongly disapproved of Tanya's dissident activities, including her relationship with me, because they endangered what he had "suffered to achieve," much like Bukharin's historian daughter objected to her half brother's public protests in the 1970s. When Bayev finally told his Gulag story four decades later, a few years before his death in 1997, more people than not were surprised by it.[5]

The great majority of survivors simply slipped back into the anonymity of society, but a significant number, like Bayev, went on to eminent Soviet careers. Though virtually unknown at the time, there were precedents even under Stalin, especially among zeks freed to fight in the war against Nazi Germany. Released with several other military officers arrested in 1937–38, Konstantin Rokossovsky, who had his fingernails yanked out and had been badly beaten by the NKVD, became one of the most successful and popular wartime generals, rising to the rank of marshal. Another freed general, Aleksandr Gorbatov, led his army all the way to Berlin, where he became head of the Soviet occupation forces in 1945. (His former cellmate occupied the same position in Vienna.)[6]

The wartime return of the rocket engineer and designer Sergei Korolev was no less consequential. Released to develop weapons against Nazi Germany, he later headed the Soviet space-exploration program. As such, considering the Soviet Union's pioneering role, the former Gulag inmate Korolev may be considered to have been the father of space travel. Nor was he alone. His colleague V.P. Glushko, who helped free Korolev in 1942 after his own release, later accomplished so much in international astronomy that a moon crater was named for him. (Unlike Korolev, whose work remained highly classified, Glushko also rose politically, becoming a member of the Communist Party Central Committee in 1976.)[7]

Of course, many more Gulag survivors rose or returned to prominence after Stalin's death than before. Several are already known to readers. Eddi Rozner recreated his jazz band and his popularity of the 1940s, though he died in 1976 embittered by his experiences and with his music eclipsed by Western rock-and-roll. Two of the Starostin brothers, Nikolai and Andrei, again became national soccer figures, now as team executives. The once beautiful ingénue Tatyana Okunevskaya resumed her acting career, though in different roles, as did Zhzhenov and another popular star, Pyotr Veliaminov. Aleksei Kapler, after serving ten years for his affair with Stalin's daughter, returned to the film world as a writer/director and host of a popular television program about movies. Anna Larina's Gulag friend, Natalya Sats, another name perhaps known to some readers, created the world-renowned Moscow Children's Theater.[8]

Such illustrious post-Gulag careers were, however, exceptions. Even after Stalin's terror was ended and its survivors freed, many gifted returnees and their children could enter public life only obliquely, by glossing over their past, adopting pseudonyms, or constructing dual existences. Bukharin's son, Yuri Larin, for example, struggled to emerge as an artist until the late 1980s, without official support and sanctioned exhibits, while maintaining public silence about his parents. Another example was his friend Yuri Aikhenvald, a handsome, extraordinarily talented man with an equally "spoiled biography," whom I met in the 1970s when his Moscow apartment was an "open house" for political and cultural nonconformists, including other returnees.

Born in 1928, Aikhenvald's life had been doubly stigmatized from the beginning—first by his paternal grandfather, Yuli, a well-known anti-Communist intellectual deported by Lenin's government in 1922; and then, on the opposing side, by his father, Aleksandr, one of the prominent Bukharinists shot by Stalin. Following his mother's arrest in 1937, Yuri Aikhenvald lived with elderly relatives, but by age fourteen was in effect an orphan on his own. In 1949, when Stalin was rounding up the now grown children of his previous victims, including Bukharin's daughter, Svetlana, Yuri Aikhenvald himself was arrested. Exiled to Kazakhstan, he was rearrested in 1951 and held in a psychiatric prison until his release in 1955.

By the 1960s, while teaching literature to high school students, Aikhenvald had developed into an outstanding poet whose best work was written "for the drawer" or published only abroad. Dissident activities, KGB persecution, and an ensuing heart attack terminated his formal employment. To support his family and achieve some public expression, Aikhenvald became the all-but-anonymous translator of popular Soviet theatrical productions, notably *Man of La Mancha* and *Cyrano de Bergerac*. Thus was a generation of Soviet theater-goers, many of them members of the Party-state elite, unknowingly entertained and edified by a former zek, himself a kind of political Don Quixote with a Cyrano-like alter ego, who took the opportunity to embed lines from his banned poems in the text.[9]

But what about the millions of other survivors freed in the 1950s? Some of their stories are known. Vadim Tumanov, the Kolyma zek freed by a traveling commission in 1956, went on to become a Siberian legend for his gold-mining feats. The geologist Pavel Vittenburg, like several other scientists, published major works without revealing that his primary research had been done in the Gulag. Another returnee poet became, using the pseudonym Roman Sef, the Russian translator of *My Fair Lady* and Walt Whitman.[10] Readers will encounter, or meet again, others further on in this book. But most of Stalin's surviving victims vanished into society without leaving recorded traces.

We can only guess, therefore, how many of them found a *kheppi end*, as Russians also say, and how many never did. When I asked returnees I knew what they thought had happened to all the others, they usually shrugged and replied, in a Russian idiom, "Even former zeks had different fates." Presumably—or we should hope—many who lived out their lives privately managed to achieve a relatively happy end, at least in the Soviet context. (Even though Kamil Ikramov's eyesight was so badly damaged in the Gulag that he could not appreciate the paintings of his friend Yuri Larin, he looked back on his return as "a happy finale" and the "beginning of a new life.") But many were not so fortunate. Some of them could be seen over the years living in homes for the aged, railway stations, and makeshift shelters, hopelessly dysfunctional and destitute.[11]

The sad end of two returnees, both admired authors, may tell us something about many unknown ones. Shalamov, once considered by some "Russia's greatest living writer," died in exceptionally lonely circumstances, an inchoate ward of the state's primitive facilities. The frail, once beautiful poet of the Leningrad blockade of 1941–44, Olga Berggolts, whose words, "No one is forgotten, nothing is forgotten," adorn its most revered monument, never recovered from the Stalinist terror. In the 1930s, her first and second husbands were executed and both of her young daughters, one an infant, died, as did the child Berggolts was carrying during her own imprisonment from 1937 to 1939. After fighting the affliction for two decades, she died of alcoholism in 1975, having lived her last years, her sister said, in "pain, wine, and loneliness."[12]

Broad generalizations about the political views of returnees are as untenable as those about their careers and personal lives. Many surviving victims blamed the entire Soviet system, beginning with Lenin, for their sufferings, a few becoming well-known, anti-Marxist religious dissidents, such as Father Dmitri Dudko, whose humanistic homilies attracted worshippers and non-worshippers to his small parish outside Moscow in the 1970s. Others returned from the Gulag so embittered or cynical they never again believed in any kind of politics or ideology. Still others, as we will see, developed various convictions that led them to the ideologically diverse dissent of the 1960s and 1970s.

On the other hand, though it may surprise readers, many surviving political victims of the Soviet 1930s and 1940s, as well as children of those who perished, joined the Communist Party, or tried to do so. (Only slightly more than half of the applicants seem to have been admitted.) They had different reasons. For some, as for many of the Party's almost 20 million members by the 1980s, membership was mainly a way of obtaining a better apartment, job, pension, and other state benefits. For others, it was an affirmation of complete exoneration. As Natalya Rykova wrote in an appeal for her mother's posthumous readmission to the Party, "Judicial rehabilitation . . . without Party rehabilitation is still not rehabilitation."[13]

But many returning victims joined, or rejoined, the Communist Party because of strong political convictions. Veteran Communists expelled from the Party when they were arrested—people like

Shatunovskaya, Snegov, Gnedin, Milchakov, and Kopelev—
believed Khrushchev was fighting, against powerful opposition, to
restore the system's original Leninist values perverted by Stalin.
They wanted to support the new leader. Having clung to a belief in
the Soviet Revolution throughout their many years in the Gulag—
they said it helped them survive "without breaking"—now, in the
approving words of a Berggolts poem, "they came first to get back
their old Party card."[14]

Nor were these new Party members only elderly people seeking
to justify their political youth of the 1920s. Children of parents
swept away by the terror, their biographies long "spoiled," also now
joined the Party. They too wanted to stand with Khrushchev and
thereby redeem their parents' lives. Among them were my friends
Roy Medvedev, whose Red Army father was formally exonerated
the day after Khrushchev's anti-Stalin speech in 1956; Mikhail
Shatrov, who had lost many relatives; Leonid Petrovsky, whose
Bukharinist father had been shot but whose grandfather was one
of the very few old Bolsheviks not arrested; and Kamil Ikramov,
the son of one of Bukharin's co-defendants. The same was the case
with Pyotr Yakir, the general's son who spent his childhood in the
Gulag, and Bulat Okudzhava, later one of the most popular Soviet
balladeers.

By the 1970s, most of them, having protested the policies of
Khrushchev's successors, had quit the Party, like Gnedin, or been
expelled, like Kopelev, Medvedev, Yakir, and Okudzhava. Gnedin's
letter of resignation spoke for all of them: "Belonging to the Party
generally contradicts the understanding I have formed over the
years of social life and of the meaning of being an individual." A
few were even rearrested, but Lev Razgon's turnabout was the most
dramatic. Still a believing Communist when he returned from the
Gulag in the 1950s, and a celebrated author during Gorbachev's
anti-Stalinist reforms of the late 1980s, Razgon nonetheless
resigned and testified against the Communist Party at the trial
staged by the post-Soviet government in 1992.

But the overwhelming majority of surviving zeks who returned to the Party remained loyally, or submissively, in its ranks for the rest of their lives. Their best-known representative was Galina Serebryakova, a strong-willed woman who had spent twenty-one years in the Gulag and whose first and second husbands, both high-ranking Communists, had been executed. Speaking at a meeting of cultural figures and officials attended by Khrushchev, she thanked the Party she had rejoined, and its leader personally, for "my second birth, my return to this world from the abyss." The "main tragedy" for all the victims who had remained "firm and faithful Leninists," she said, had not been the loss of their children or the physical torture, which had left "five scars on my breasts," but the "fate of the proletarian revolution, the fate of the Party."[15]

Serebryakova never seemed to waver in this sense of the "main tragedy," even after Khrushchev's inglorious overthrow and the rollback of his anti-Stalinist reforms. She continued to be a prolific writer on sanctioned Marxist-Leninist subjects whose books were published in mass editions. For this, Serebryakova was held in contempt by many Soviet intellectuals who had never suffered, and also by some returnees who thought she represented the "generation of the deceived," though I thought her story and similar ones were more complex.[16]

There was, to take a case that particularly interested me, the return of Bukharin's personal secretary, Semyon Lyandres. Like Serebryakova and thousands of other victims, he remained a "believing Communist" to the end. I learned about Lyandres' post-Gulag life from his son, Julian Semyonov, an enormously successful author of spy and police novels who patterned his adventurous lifestyle on Hemingway. Julian insisted it was unfair to expect Stalinist victims of his father's and Serebryakova's generation, or their grown children (no doubt with himself in mind), to "go into the political wilderness" a second time, which is how they saw life outside the Party.[17] Most Communist returnees apparently agreed, though a few did not.

That was only one of many political disagreements among Stalin's surviving victims, Communist and non-Communist. Solzhenitsyn was at the center of several. In 1962, freed zeks reacted in heatedly different ways to his path-breaking *One Day in the Life of Ivan Denisovich*, some insisting he portrayed the camps too benignly, others too harshly. The most profound dispute developed between Solzhenitsyn and the writer he initially embraced as another "true son of the Gulag," Shalamov. But while Solzhenitsyn espoused the possibility of personal and moral redemption in the Gulag experience, Shalamov insisted there was only dehumanization and death. As Solzhenitsyn's fame and message spread, his onetime "brother" increasingly viewed him as a "polisher of reality," even, it was reported, a "mendacious political manipulator."[18]

Solzhenitsyn's famously cantankerous nature—he had "ideological" fallings-out with several former zeks, including Kopelev, his close friend in the Gulag—was a major factor, but there were other political conflicts as well. Ginzburg, who refused to rejoin the Party, came to despise Milchakov, her friend in Kolyma, believing he had reacquired his pre-arrest attitudes as a high official along with his Party card. She thought, though it was not fully true, that "along with his prison clothes he had discarded any relationship with us" and "neatly repaired the broken thread of his life. He had knotted the two ends together securely, joined up 1937 and 1954 and thrown away everything in between." Nor were such disputes short-lived. Many years later, a war of words broke out between rival organizations of former zeks over which was truly representative.[19]

Of course, most of Stalin's victims of all political outlooks hated him, but even here disagreements emerged. After the end of the Soviet Union, Father Dudko and Vladimir Karpov, another prisoner released for the war against Hitler's Germany and later a head of the Soviet Writers Union, became defenders of

Stalin's state-building role in history. And for the same nationalist reasons, Marshal Rokossovsky, who had eight teeth knocked out by the NKVD in 1937, was said to have refused to participate in Khrushchev's anti-Stalin campaign because "for me, Comrade Stalin is sacred."[20]

Regardless of their individual paths after the Gulag, collectively the millions of returnees were a major new factor in Soviet life, especially following the terror-ridden conformity of the Stalin years. Their common experiences, needs, and demands created problems and conflicts that compelled responses, compassionate or otherwise, from the political-administrative system under Khrushchev.

When Ginzburg wrote to Kliment Voroshilov, an unrepentant Stalinist still in the leadership, "During these years, I lost everything,"[21] she spoke for most returnees. Though some were determined to make up for lost time by experiencing whatever limited conveniences and consumer pleasures existed in the 1950s—many, for example, had never sent a telegram or seen television—the great majority wanted the basic elements of a new, or renewed, life: family, medical care, an apartment, a job or pension, financial compensation for their years in captivity, and the return of property confiscated when they were sentenced.

The government's general response was an unwritten but often spoken social contract: "We will meet your elementary needs and leave you in peace, but you must not make political demands or clamor about the past." (When released, many survivors had been warned not to talk about what had happened to them.) In the end, what the post-Stalin government did, and did not do, for his surviving victims was shaped by politics and the nature of the bureaucratic system, but also by the austerity and scarcity that characterized Soviet life in general.

Official agencies could do little for families torn apart by years of repression. They helped some returnees find their relatives, but even that was done mostly by friends, other family members, and occasionally the Red Cross. Making the problem worse, the NKVD had lied since the 1930s about the death of loved ones, a practice continued for several years by its successor organization, the KGB. To conceal the mass executions, Stalinist "justice" contrived a false sentence, "ten years without the right of correspondence." In reality, it meant the victim had been shot.

Some people deciphered the cruel fiction, a few recalling with tears the poet Aleksandr Blok's line about the Gates of Heaven, "No one would ever return." Occasionally a NKVD agent or prosecutor, after stating the official euphemism, told a spouse, "You can remarry." But many people believed their loved ones were still alive in some remote camp. Anton Antonov-Ovseyenko's sister, Galina, herself a zek in the 1940s, was certain their father was also somewhere in the Gulag, but "Papa doesn't have the right to correspond." Aleksandr Arosev's wife and daughter, the actress Olga, learned of his execution only in 1955. Even the well-connected Boris Yefimov accepted false assurances about his brother given to him personally by Stalin's hanging judge, Vasily Ulrikh.[22] As a result, many relatives expected their loved ones to return after ten years, in 1947 or 1948, and then after Stalin died in 1953. Some women waited in vain for their husbands until their own deaths.

The saga of children affected by the terror also dragged on for many years. Those old enough at the time to understand their parents were arrested as "enemies of the people" had faced agonizing choices between family loyalty and their own futures in Stalin's Soviet Union. When Olga Aroseva learned her older sister had renounced their father to avoid being expelled from the Young Communist League, she hit her. As Olga later explained, "The pain I felt for my father lived on in me all these years."[23]

She never joined any Communist organization, even though membership would have furthered her acting career. Similar decisions sometimes alienated surviving family members forever. As for the children who believed their fathers had actually been guilty, and who strove for years to conform in order "to cleanse the stain," Khrushchev's revelations made many of them deeply ashamed of their own lives. Others continued to conceal the fact of their parents' arrest, and some do so even today.[24]

Less traumatically, Vasily Aksyonov visited his mother in exile in Magadan when he was a teenager, but by the 1950s, back on the "mainland," he had become absorbed in "my own youthful affairs," while his mother withdrew into her second family. The alienation continued after her release. By then an author whose fame was spreading in the Soviet Union, Vasily felt even more estranged from his returnee father, Pavel Aksyonov, recoiling from his "unclean, obscure odors," though eventually he reconciled with both parents. Similarly, Yelena Bonner, later the wife of the great liberal dissident Andrei Sakharov, resented her long-absent mother's attempt to resume a maternal role, her obsession with her Gulag past, and her meetings with other former zeks, including the gentle and caring Igor Pyatnitsky.[25]

Very young children who had vanished into orphanages and foster homes were usually found, though some were not and are still missing today. (Reuniting family members separated decades ago by the terror is the premise of a contemporary Russian reality television program called *Wait for Me*.) The wife of Vasily Blyukher, the marshal beaten to death, survived, for example, but could not find their youngest son.[26] Reunions between children and freed parents who had never really known each other required wrenching adjustments on both sides.

Anna Larina and her son Yuri were separated for almost twenty years after her arrest in 1937, when he was less than a year old. In 1954, having learned that his mother was alive and in

Siberian exile, he wrote to her from his orphanage: "Dear Mama! I do not understand everything in my life. Why did I leave my own home? Where is my papa? I beg you to answer." The life-changing answers had to wait until 1956, when Yuri was able to travel to Larina's remote place of confinement, where he finally learned that his father was a Soviet founder and still an infamous "enemy of the people"—Nikolai Bukharin. Within a few days, mother and son bonded for life. And by 1959, Anna had returned to Moscow with Yuri and her two younger children, Nadya and Misha, from her Gulag husband.

But there were also unhappy reunions. A young daughter reacted negatively to her returning mother, who "looked like a beggar woman" and whose post-Gulag "moods" pushed her further away. The daughter always "remained, in her heart, an orphan." Another young woman was never able to understand what her mother had experienced in the camps until many years later, after the former inmate's death, she traveled to Magadan and saw mass graves just below the permafrost. Similarly, enlightened about what happened to her mother by her own subsequent experiences, Bonner too later regretted the "impassable barrier between us." Okudzhava had a similar experience with his mother, who returned an "entirely different" person, and about which he later wrote a famous short story.[27]

As these examples suggest, returnees often found it difficult to reestablish close relationships not only with their children but with other family members who had remained free. Sometimes the reason was simply differences wrought by time. Thus, Ginzburg's sister "turned out to be a complete stranger," and apparently remained one. A more profound, though perhaps rarely spoken, reason was the stark contrast between a life lost and one lived. I heard several versions of the feeling expressed by the cousin of a returnee in Grossman's documentary-like novel, *Everything Flows*: "The news of his cousin's arrival was shocking . . . because it made the whole of his own life, in all its truth and untruth, appear before him."[28] Given those contrasting experiences, we can only imagine the reunion between the longtime zek, Lev Netto, and his younger soccer star brother, Igor, whom he had not seen in thirteen years.

Marriage, the most intricate of relationships, was, of course, severely tested by the terror, even when both the husband and wife were imprisoned. The full estrangement—psychological, emotional, and political—of Aksyonov's parents by the time they were freed in the 1950s, both committed Communists when they were "taken" in 1937, was well known in returnee and intellectual circles, but it was only one of many marriages destroyed by Stalin's repressions. Separated for decades by mass arrests in the countryside, rural couples also turned out to be "alien" to each other. Their return only finalized the "disintegration" of those families as well.[29]

When just one spouse had been arrested, usually though not always the husband, reunions ranged from happy to tragic. There were countless instances of long marital faithfulness. Yevgeny Gnedin's wife, Nadezhda, not only waited steadfastly for him throughout his decade in prisons and camps but then voluntarily joined him in exile in Kazakhstan, a sacrifice that put her at constant risk. Some husbands also were heroic. One waited fifteen years for his wife while raising her arrested sister's children. As his wife recalled after her return, "By the standards of recent times, it would have been entirely normal for Adolf to remarry in 1940, for the children to be put in a home."[30]

But the long terror also caused spousal renunciations, which the authorities encouraged, divorces, and new marriages. Marshal Semyon Budyonny, one of Stalin's most pompous and inept military men, immediately disowned his arrested wife and had their marriage annulled. Stalin's longtime chief-of-staff, Aleksandr Poskrebyshev, remarried soon after his wife was taken. The husband of the actress Tatyana Okunevskaya renounced her, remarried, and evicted her mother from their apartment. Some victims returned after many years to discover that their spouses had changed identities and vanished, along with the children. Not all returnees cared, as Shalamov famously explained: "I wouldn't want to go back to my family now. They wouldn't understand me, they couldn't . . . No man should see or know the things I have seen and known."[31]

Women left alone were especially vulnerable to the harshness of Soviet life. "The doors of all 'decent' apartments," we are told by another great widow-memoirist, Nadezhda Mandelstam, "were now firmly slammed in their faces."[32] Many were unable to find work to support themselves and their children. And yet, a considerable number, like Gnedin's wife, remained steadfast, often without even knowing if their husbands were still alive. Such fidelity was not always rewarded. Desperate for companionship, and uncertain about wives left behind, men in mixed-sex camps and exile frequently found new mates. When one wife waited ten years for her husband only to find him living with another woman, she was unforgiving: "After enduring so much for ten years, coping with so many of my own hardships, was it possible to count on any kind of masculine support? No, and again no!"[33]

The impact of the terror on marriages was often so traumatic that close observers could not apportion responsibility for their breakup. Wives sometimes blamed arrested husbands, not the Stalinist system, for the stigma that attached to them as well. Shalamov's wife deserted him to escape the shadow of the Gulag, while he, utterly transformed by his camp experience, no longer wished to live with her either. Solzhenitsyn's first wife, Natalya Reshetovskaya, remarried during his long imprisonment, but returned to him after his release. A friend thought, "She's home again, all is forgotten," but it was not so simple. Reemerging as a "true son of the Gulag" in his writing, Solzhenitsyn soon left Reshetovskaya for another woman.[34] (Hence Reshetovskaya's embittered instruction that I keep her memoirs "from the KGB and from friends of Aleksandr Isayevich [Solzhenitsyn].")

Many returnees who found no family waiting for them soon remarried. (Having seen fellow prisoners left for days where they dropped dead, Ginzburg, who remarried at sixty-three, explained, "At least when you're married, someone will bury you straight away.")[35] Very often the new spouse had also been a victim, as in the marriages of Anna Larina, Igor Pyatnitsky, Aikhenvald, Razgon, Pyotr Yakir, and Antonov-Ovseyenko. In some instances, the relationship had begun in the Gulag. But others grew from a feeling among returnees that only another former zek could fully understand them or the stigma they bore. That was why many children of victims also inter-married, sometimes causing anxious concern in their parents, as did Yakir's daughter, Irina, and the bard Yuli Kim; Shatrov and his first wife; Aroseva and her first husband; and Kopelev's daughter, Lena.

Male returnees, however, frequently sought new lives with younger women who could give them what the Gulag had cost them, including children. Solzhenitsyn left Reshetovskaya for a woman twenty-two years his junior. Aleksei Snegov, whose political role at Khrushchev's side is featured in the next chapter, had a similar post-Gulag marriage. Another former zek who also lived into his nineties, Oleg Volkov, probably expressed the feelings of most of these aging men: "A young woman was able to instill in a sixty-year-old man . . . belief in his possibilities, to create conditions enabling him to forget about his age and with youthful energy plunge back into his work."[36] Most female returnees, on the other hand, never found new husbands, adding to the large number of Soviet unmarried women that had resulted from World War II.

The government had no part, of course, in these intimate aspects of a returnee's life, but nor did it do anything for Gulag survivors suffering from psychological "post-camp syndrome."

Like Holocaust survivors, many former zeks were tormented by memories of what they had endured. Even a seemingly well-adjusted woman, also age ninety, rose on her deathbed to exclaim, "I must go. The guards are waiting to escort me."[37] She was not the only one who could not forget. Everyday reminders of their terrible experiences—a loud noise, a sudden knock on the door, the harsh tone of an official's voice—could trigger panic attacks in Gulag survivors, but the Soviet mental-health profession did not even recognize the condition. Distraught returnees sought comfort instead in circles of other victims, who were "like a family." Some even expressed nostalgia for the survivalist comradeship of the Gulag.[38] How many ever found inner peace is unknown.

Despite statutes enacted under Khrushchev, nor did more than a few returnees receive anything approaching financial compensation for their years of deprivation and suffering. The standard official recompense was a mere two months of their pre-arrest salary. Compounding their loss, few regained the personal property almost always confiscated when they were arrested or sentenced, such as apartments, books, and other household possessions, though partial compensation was occasionally granted by courts.[39] Among the returnees I knew, some never even recovered family photographs. Anna Larina did not have a single photograph of herself with Bukharin, even though scores had been taken by a relative who was a famous portraitist. (His son destroyed the negatives after Bukharin's arrest.) A hat saved by his former nanny was the only memento Ikramov had of his beloved father, prompting his wife to remark, "What kind of country is it when all that remains of a person is a Panama hat?"

Victims and their relatives often asked what had become of the enormous quantities of personal possessions confiscated during the Stalinist terror. "How did those killers divide up the things, furniture, shoes, pots and pans of their victims?" Plisetskaya later wondered. "At night, at dawn, or in broad daylight? Did their fat wives squeeze into other people's used clothing, or did they drag everything to the flea market?"[40]

We now know. Many personal possessions were lost in frenzied searches that accompanied the mass arrests or were burned in prison furnaces, as happened with unpublished works by the great writer Isaak Babel, the renowned geneticist Nikolai Vavilov, and Bukharin, one of whose final book manuscripts is still missing. "A soot-stained chimney," it has been reported, "sprinkled Moscow with the ash of incinerated manuscripts" from the NKVD's Lubyanka Prison.[41] Scores of incinerators no doubt were also flaming in provincial Lubyankas across the Soviet Union.

But much was taken by the NKVD for itself. In Moscow, the pillaging was well-organized. (Lubyanka had an extraordinary library based on confiscated books.) In those years of mass scarcity, ranking secret-police officers eagerly moved their families into the furnished apartments of their victims. Many smaller items were distributed to subordinates in NKVD warehouses or sold in special stores that sprang up in Moscow and other large cities in the late 1930s. (Fifty years later, a few pieces of china with Bukharin's initials, manufactured in the 1920s in his honor, were anonymously returned to his widow; and one of the many missing paintings Bukharin had done over the years, purchased by an American tourist in a Moscow antique shop in 1989, turned up in Oregon.) Most of the highly placed officials who inherited "arrested property," like a fine apartment, evidently felt no guilt, only "a genuine, secret power that came close to fate and divine providence."[42]

In provincial Soviet towns, where NKVD arresting officers were often brutish young men hastily recruited from orphanages, the looting was more chaotic. Even during the formal procedures of "arrest and search," they fought over whatever they found, from money, lamps, and kitchen utensils to threadbare clothes.[43] The "confiscations" were so widespread that people fearing arrest sometimes gave possessions to friends or hid them. Most of it also disappeared, but there were exceptions. A few of Bukharin's paintings and photographs of former premier Rykov were hidden by friends in 1937 until Anna Larina and Rykov's daughter, Natalya, returned. And family documents concealed under a floorboard in his apartment by a doomed leader of Abkhazia, then part of Soviet Georgia, were retrieved twenty years later by a relative who knew the secret.[44]

One episode reflected the wanton nature of the terror-era looting. Andrei Vyshinsky, Stalin's chief prosecutor at the Moscow Show Trials of the late 1930s, took for himself the prized dacha, land, and funds associated with the property of one of his own victims, the once prominent Party and state official Leonid Serebryakov. Knowing the outcome, Vyshinsky began the "legal" transfer of the property while Serebryakov's trial was under way. Vyshinsky died in 1954—in New York, where he was serving as Soviet ambassador to the United Nations—but when Serebryakov's daughter later returned from the Gulag, the Inquisitor's family was still living in the dacha.[45]

Nonetheless, the Soviet government under Khrushchev did meet the basic needs of most of Stalin's surviving victims. The majority of them eventually received living space, a job or a pension, health and dental care—severe periodontal disease caused by years of malnutrition made dentures especially important—and other modest benefits of the expanding Soviet welfare system. Some were initially assigned cramped communal apartments but later given their own units as Khrushchev's construction of new apartment buildings progressed; and a general pension reform in 1956 tacitly expanded the definition of time in the workplace to include years of forced labor.[46]

Recovering those benefits of full citizenship was not, however, automatic or easy. Having been "legally" convicted, returnees needed official exoneration, or "rehabilitation," as it was termed, which most of their release documents—amnesties and pardons—

had not bestowed. Without such status, many victims could not obtain the "clean"internal passport enabling them to reside in large cities, even their hometowns. Obtaining the "sacred" certificate of personal rehabilitation, which typically stated that no crime had actually been committed and which was supposed to delete their "dark past," or posthumously that of relatives who had perished, involved another case-by-case bureaucratic process.[47]

Once again, it was easiest for survivors who had influential help. For aged Communist returnees, the most active "intervenors" were a bare handful of Lenin-era Bolsheviks Stalin had spared, in particular Grigory Petrovsky (Leonid's grandfather), Yelena Stasova, Gleb Krzhizhanovsky, and Vyacheslav Karpinsky. They were tragic figures in their own way. Now elderly, all three had been personally close to Lenin, and all three had watched as most of their comrades (and his), whom they knew were innocent, were executed as traitors, assassins, and saboteurs. We can only imagine the mixed feelings of fear, relief, and guilt that tormented their long lives at liberty under Stalin.

Grigory Petrovsky's fate was especially tragic. Both of his sons were killed in 1941—the Bukharinist Pyotr shot in a provincial prison soon after the German invasion, his younger son, an army commander, at the front. Unable to bear the loss, their mother, Domenika, suffered a fatal heart attack a month later. Previously, after a "harsh" conversation with Stalin, Petrovsky had been removed as head of the Soviet Ukrainian government. He was alone and unemployable until the director of Moscow's Museum of the Revolution, an old friend, gave him refuge as his deputy.

There Petrovsky remained—except when he accompanied the wartime evacuation of Lenin's body—until Stalin died, doing what little he could for his widowed daughter-in-law and young grandson. Stalinist authorities refused to permit them to live with Petrovsky, so he found them temporary sanctuary in a provincial orphanage, she as a teacher and her son as a ward. Eventually, Petrovsky managed to bring them back to Moscow, where they lived alone in one room and where Leonid, a future Soviet historian and dissident, trained to be a lathe operator.[48] After Stalin's death, Petrovsky, his standing as one of "Lenin's close comrades-in-arms" restored, began helping Communist returnees obtain their certificates of rehabilitation and post-Gulag benefits.

Thousands of people in various cultural professions had also been arrested, and a considerable number of those survivors were helped by other establishment figures. Their "intervenors" included famous writers whom the terror had somehow by-passed, such as Ilya Ehrenburg, Konstantin Simonov, Aleksandr Tvardovsky, and even, in the months before he committed suicide, Stalin's former literary commissar, Aleksandr Fadeyev. The posthumous exoneration of major cultural figures who had not returned was no less important because their convictions as "enemies of the state" continued to be a prohibition on the revival of their pioneering, pre-Stalinist achievements.

Such was the case of the theatrical director Vsevolod Meyerhold, whose torture readers will recall. In 1955, an appeal for his rehabilitation was put in the hands of a new prosecutor, Boris Ryazhsky. Young, inexperienced, and idealistic, Ryazhsky had already been shocked by his reinvestigation of prominent political victims, including blood he found on the pages of one defendant's signed confession. Meyerhold's files, however, involved the cultural world of the 1920s, a history entirely unknown to Ryazhsky. His report resulted in Meyerhold's full rehabilitation, but also his own discovery of those still largely forbidden years, an education he received first-hand from Ehrenburg and other living artists from that era.[49]

To overcome institutional opposition to his rehabilitation policy, Khrushchev had given Ryazhsky and several other young prosecutors a "green light," an "open road to all information," in special cases. Most of Stalin's living and dead victims, however, were not so prominent or fortunate. For them, obtaining the "sacred" document remained a protracted, grudging process frequently controlled by unsympathetic bureaucrats. Nonetheless, between 1954 and Khrushchev's overthrow in 1964, 700,000 to 800,000 victims of Stalin's terror were officially rehabilitated.[50] Millions more had to wait two decades for another Soviet reform leader.

—∞—

Compared to the twenty years that followed, Khrushchev's leadership favored returnees, but reactions to them in the sprawling officialdom and society were far from uniform. Some officials were supportive, but many were not. They viewed former zeks "with suspicion," rehabilitation as "something rotten," and did not trust people with an "unclean past." (Especially unclean in their eyes were surviving relatives of the founders of the Soviet Union whom Stalin had branded arch-enemies of the nation, including Bukharin's widow and children, and Rykov's daughter.) One official spoke for many others when he warned a rehabilitated zek, "The mark was removed, but the stain remained."[51]

Such Party and state officials created obstacles to the return of the victims, from their release to their rehabilitation. Even though laws mandated positive actions, bureaucrats frequently refused survivors the documents they needed; courts ruled against their claims; state employers rejected their applications; academic directors restricted their research; and regional Party bosses targeted editors who had "a mania for justice." No matter Khrushchev's policy at the top, lesser officials were in administrative positions to do real harm. One returnee so despaired of finding work he tried to be returned to the Gulag; and the poet Anna Barkova, who had already served two terms, was sent back for no reason other than malice.[52]

Reactions in society also varied. Returnees told me many stories of welcoming kindness, not only on the part of family and friends but of other people. Virtual strangers gave destitute survivors shelter, clothing, food, and money. On another level, the emerging liberal intelligentsia and many young people of the 1950s and 1960s embraced returning zeks as "something romantic," as "torch-bearers of truth and integrity," and gave them a "hero's reception."[53] The publication I mentioned earlier about Yevgeny Gnedin, for instance, was entitled "The Poem's Hero."

But many ordinary citizens reacted to former zeks with unconcealed suspicion and hostility, as had perhaps most Soviet people when victims were taken years before. Plisetskaya remembered being shocked when a janitor, observing her father's arrest, shouted, "Can't wait for all you bastards to be shot," but his response was not uncommon. Stalin had died, but after decades of indoctrination, "he still lives," as was often said, "inside us." Not even official exoneration redeemed returnees in the eyes of people who were certain, "There's no smoke without fire." Indeed, those widespread attitudes were reinforced after Stalin's death by mass outbreaks of theft, rape, and murder resulting from the 1953 amnesty of actual criminals.[54] In the aftermath, many Soviet citizens saw no difference between released political and criminal prisoners.

One social group did have reason to be fearful. Millions of people had been implicated in some way in Stalin's nearly twenty-five-year terror, from Party and state apparatchiki who implemented his orders and hundreds of thousands, perhaps millions, of NKVD personnel who arrested, tortured, executed, and guarded victims to countless petty informers and eager slanderers spawned by the blood-ridden plague. Millions of other citizens had been implicated indirectly, inheriting the positions, possessions, and even wives and children of the vanished. Two generations had built lives and careers on the terror's consequences, which killed but also "corrupted the living."[55]

Despite the pervasive and paralyzing fear, some Soviet citizens had, of course, resisted complicity in the terror. There were school teachers who postponed examinations for children traumatized by their parents' arrest, and "many wonderful people," as Shatrov later recalled, who gave orphans sanctuaries; state employers who hired stigmatized spouses; inhabitants of small towns and villages who mailed desperate notes victims had scribbled to loved ones and tossed from Gulag-bound trains; a woman doctor who served voluntarily in a Kolyma hospital; the widow of the classic writer Maksim Gorky, Yekaterina Peshkova, who helped prisoners until her relief organization was shut down in 1938; even a few prosecutors, NKVD interrogators, and camp guards who showed compassion to victims.[56]

And in spite of the great risks to themselves, a significant number of prominent, well-placed cultural, academic, and scientific figures tried to save their arrested colleagues. Their efforts were usually in vain, and they too often fell victim, though not always. The nuclear physicist Pyotr Kapitsa, himself highly vulnerable, intervened directly with Stalin on behalf of his young protégé Lev Landau. Both survived to win Nobel prizes in the 1960s. Similarly, at no less risk to himself, the eminent biologist Vladimir Engelgardt probably saved the life of Tanya's father, Aleksandr Bayev, his onetime protégé. During Bayev's many years in the Gulag, he was permitted to work as a camp doctor, rather than at hard labor, due to Engelgardt's persistent appeals on his behalf. In turn, Bayev saved the lives of many other zeks.[57]

But by 1956, as the return from the Gulag grew into a mass exodus, a profound antagonism was unfolding between two Soviet communities—the victims of the terror and their victimizers. As Akhmatova, whose son, Lev Gumilyov, was finally released that year, foresaw, "Now those who were arrested will return, and two Russias will be eyeball to eyeball: the one that put people in the camps and the one put there." The first, she added, "are now trembling for their names, positions, apartments, dachas. The whole calculation was that no one would return."[58]

Widespread conflicts were inevitable. Most returnees passively accepted the government's assistance, but a significant number wanted more—real compensation, fuller political disclosures, official punishment of those responsible for their suffering. Some victims took action, including lawsuits and campaigns to expose people in their professions or neighborhoods who had been secret police agents and informers. Others had long dreamt of a Monte Cristo-like revenge. Dumas' story of meticulously planned and executed vengeance in early nineteenth-century France was told and re-told in the camps to prisoners who had not read the novel.

Few, if any, actually took such extreme steps. The Medvedev brothers, Roy and Zhores, tracked down the person who had denounced their father. The man was now a professor at the same Leningrad University where Roy was studying. The young twins secretly scrutinized his career and stalked him, but did nothing more. Shortly after his release, Aleksandr Milchakov found himself alone outside the office of Lazar Kaganovich, Stalin's close accomplice in the terror. He considered charging in, but walked on. Their reticence was not forgiveness. Lev Razgon claimed that by the time he returned from the Gulag, his "hatred, bitterness, and vengeful feelings" had passed.[59] But thirty-five years later, his zealous literary pursuit of victimizers continued to remind a mutual friend of the Count of Monte Cristo.

Some victims, on the other hand, adopted a position still being debated in Russia today—that "no one was guilty" because the Stalinist terror had deprived everyone of real choice. That outlook may help to explain two unusual stories in the history of the terror and its aftermath. In the 1950s, Yuri Tomsky, the youngest son of one of Stalin's leading political victims, had a brief but public romance with the late dictator's daughter, Svetlana.[60] When word of the affair reached returnee circles, some former zeks, as was Tomsky himself, were angered by his conduct.

More long-running was the relationship between the actress Olga Aroseva and Molotov, another of Stalin's closest accomplices. Initially, Aroseva resented Molotov for having abandoned her father, whom he still called "a very close friend of mine," along with herself, her sister, and their mother. But through warm personal relations with Molotov's wife, Polina—readers will remember her arrest and early release—Aroseva's feelings toward him grew into some kind of forgiveness, and she wished him a long life. When the old man died in 1986, a widower at age ninety-six, she helped arrange the funeral.[61]

Years later, I witnessed an even more unusual instance of forgiveness. In the early 1990s, I found the daughter of the man who had been Bukharin's NKVD interrogator in Lubyanka Prison in 1937, and who was himself later shot. At their mutual request, I introduced her to Bukharin's widow. Anna Larina immediately put the interrogator's terribly anxious daughter, now in her sixties, at ease with four words: "They were both victims." But nothing more general should be concluded from that meeting. Very few returnees, apart from her friends Gnedin and Ikramov, who did "not want revenge" but rather that "children and grandchildren of hangmen do not become hangmen or the victims of hangmen," shared Larina's magnanimous spirit and lack of bitterness. Many more agreed with Antonov-Ovseyenko that the difference between "victims and hangmen" was absolute and "eternal."[62]

As Gulag victims came home, their confrontations with *palachi*—a word that can be translated as "hangmen," "executioners," or "butchers"—became more frequent. Some face-to-face encounters were intentional, among them ones involving the fifty-five-year-old Fadeyev, Stalin's former head of the Soviet Writers Union, on the eve of his suicide in May 1956. A handsome, debonair, once-talented novelist, he had served, in his own words, as "Stalin's satrap," even rising to membership on the Party Central Committee while scores of writers he knew personally disappeared. A few now suddenly reappeared and sought him out. Some came only to seek his help. (Known for occasional acts of kindness, Fadeyev was not among Stalin's worst accomplices.) But Khrushchev's revelations at the Party congress in February had been a "stern sentence" on Fadeyev's life, and seeing victims after so many years made the verdict even worse. Consider a letter he received from a writer who had spent nineteen years in the Gulag: "I recently returned from there—there from where not everyone returns ... Of course, I am not the same Vanka Makaryev you knew, but a sick, crippled old man."[63] Exactly why Fadeyev shot himself to death remains unknown. His chronic alcoholism was a factor, but so was the return of the victims.

Unlike with Fadeyev, most confrontations were unintended encounters in public places. One returnee dropped dead upon coming face-to-face with the man who had tortured him, while another saw "fear of death" in the eyes of his NKVD interrogator. Encountering her victim, a woman informer was left paralyzed by a stroke. Awkward meetings occurred at professional institutions, where returning survivors saw colleagues they knew had contributed to their arrest, some now in positions of authority. They reacted variously. One spit on his betrayer; another refused to shake the hand of his; yet another pretended not to know.[64] Those were low-level consequences of the return of the victims, but similar ones were unfolding at the top of the Soviet political system.

—⁓—

Another ramification of the great return was moving events in the same political direction. Even in conditions of repressive censorship, experiences of that magnitude were bound to find cultural expression. The irrepressible percolation of the "camp theme," as it soon became known, from the lower depths of Soviet society into unofficial and then sanctioned culture was an important and lasting development of Khrushchev's Thaw. Now more widely studied than when I first observed it in Moscow in the late 1970s and early 1980s, Gulag culture emerged across the spectrum from language, music, and literature to paintings and sculptures.

Zeks returning from the "little zone," as they called the archipelago of camps, to the "big zone," as they termed submissive Soviet society, brought with them a jargon commonplace in the Gulag but prohibited in public discourse under Stalin. Some people were deeply offended by its coarseness and seeming romanticization of the criminal world, but I heard it spoken casually by many Muscovites, especially intellectuals and young people. Within a few years, it was the subject of entire dictionaries published abroad.

Gulag vernacular spread even more widely through prison-related songs, which, an observer recalled, "marched into towns on the backs of 'rehabilitated' offenders." They were performed or adapted by popular bards, two of them, Bulat Okudzhava and Yuli Kim, sons of victims. None of the songs could pass official censorship, but due to the "tape-recorder revolution" of those years young people without any direct experience with the terror were singing Kim's songs about informers and lines like, "You have ravaged my precious youth. Damn you, Kolyma!"[65] (One musical returnee did have an official impact. The jazzman Eddi Rozner was told by the Minister of Culture, "We are rehabilitating the saxophone.")[66]

Visual art, on the other hand, was less portable and thus more easily prohibited, but judging by what I saw and was told, a considerable number of Gulag-related paintings, drawings, and even sculptures were seen at that time in apartments, studios, and, in one instance, on the lawn of a zek who remained in Siberia.[67] Such works, virtually all of them done by returnees, ranged from large oil canvases depicting arrests and life and death in the camps to small graphic drawings of the torture of naked women prisoners. One remarkable former zek, Yevfrosiniya Kersnovskaya, drew illustrations of almost every episode in her voluminous memoirs of life in the camps and after. The existence of such art was known in select circles by the 1970s, but its first public showings in the late 1980s were a sensation.[68]

Meanwhile, returnees had begun to put their personal experiences in prose and poetry. Most of it remained part of the underground, or "catacomb," culture until the Gorbachev period, but not all of it. A small wave of Gulag-related writings made its way into official publications soon after Khrushchev's 1956 speech, well before the flood unleashed by his public anti-Stalinist revelations in late 1961 and highlighted by Solzhenitsyn's *One Day in the Life of Ivan Denisovich*. Camp literature would soon grow into a substantial published genre posing searing questions about the Soviet past and present—about the nation's "dreadful and bloody wound," as even the government newspaper acknowledged.[69]

None of those developments after 1953 should be understood apart from what was still a harshly repressive political system. To have a larger impact, they required initiatives at the top. Nonetheless, the social and cultural dimensions of the return of so many victims were creating pressure "downstairs" for a response "upstairs," in the imagery of a Soviet journalist, more radical than Khrushchev's remarks had been at the 1956 Party congress. As archive documents later revealed, even Khrushchev's guarded revelations had already generated an "elemental wave of protest and hope, of pleading and faith in the restoration of justice." When the political response came in the early 1960s, this "muffled rumble of subterranean strata," as Solzhenitsyn felt it to be, was both a causal and divisive factor in the struggles that followed.[70]

CHAPTER 4

The Rise and Fall of "Khrushchev's Zeks"

It was Khrushchev who discovered Yakir, praised him, encouraged him. He discovered Solzhenitsyn and promoted him—that scum.

—Yuri Solomentsev, Politburo Meeting, 1972

Solzhenitsyn served time in prison as punishment for a flagrant violation of Soviet law, and was rehabilitated. But how was he rehabilitated? He was rehabilitated by two people—Shatunovskaya and Snegov.

—Leonid Brezhnev, Politburo Meeting, 1974

Aleksandr Solzhenitsyn, whose writings about his experiences brought him a Nobel Prize and made his name known around the world, became the Gulag's most famous survivor, but he is not the only one who deserves our attention. Though virtually unknown, other returnees played important political roles under Khrushchev. Among them were former zeks who influenced Kremlin policy in crucial ways and thereby helped save the lives of thousands of their fellow victims.

Unlike in several other Communist countries where bloody purges had occurred, no survivor of Stalin's terror ever returned to the Soviet political leadership. Everyone who might have done so had long since been killed. Only Aleksandr Milchakov, the one-time Young Communist leader, seems to have hoped for a high political appointment, and a heart attack in 1956 ended that aspiration. A number of returnees were given positions in the ruling Party apparatus, but only at lower levels, either because of their health or because "the stain remained." Several reported being "trusted by the Party," but, like Willy Loman in Arthur Miller's *Death of a Salesman*, not well trusted.[1]

Many more freed zeks did make their way into the large Soviet administrative class, or nomenklatura, that managed the state bureaucratic system. Some even became *nachalniki*, or "bosses," as Russians say. They included, as readers know, Marshal Rokossovsky and several generals, the space pioneer Korolev, and Academician Bayev. Others became directors of the country's most prestigious institutes of economics and literature. Even the head of the museum on the iconic revolutionary cruiser Aurora, whose guns had backed Lenin's takeover in 1917, was a former zek Solzhenitsyn had known in the Gulag, Boris Burkovsky.[2] In the late 1970s, in an informal survey, I asked acquaintances if any of their superiors had "sat" under Stalin. Many answered affirmatively.

But the most important political role belonged to a small group of returnees who unexpectedly appeared close to the center of Kremlin power soon after their release. Before spending many years in Stalin's camps and exile, Olga Shatunovskaya and Aleksei Snegov had been middle-level Communist Party officials, and Valentina Pikina, a leader of the Young Communist organization. Now in their fifties, they were freed early, in 1953 and 1954, and quickly became, due to personal ties to the two leaders, members of the extended entourage of Khrushchev and Anastas Mikoyan, his closest ally.

By the time I began this project in Moscow in the 1970s, Shatunovskaya and Snegov had long since been banished from the corridors of power, but they remained legendary figures among the Gulag survivors I knew. Both were spoken of, sometimes with expressions of personal gratitude, as heroes, even saviors; and both later became important sources for the uncensored histories of the terror written by Roy Medvedev and Anton Antonov-Ovseyenko. Shatunovskaya and Snegov, along with Pikina and others, were referred to as "Khrushchev's zeks," both by their admirers and by anti-Khrushchev officials who hated them.

Khrushchev and Mikoyan clearly trusted those recently exonerated "enemies of the people" more than they did the Stalinist officials who still dominated the Party and state apparatuses. By 1955, on Khrushchev's personal authority, Shatunovskaya and Pikina sat on the Party's supreme judiciary body, the Central Control Committee, which oversaw rehabilitation policy. Snegov and Yevsei Shirvindt, another returnee, held high positions in the Ministry of the Interior, which administered the Gulag itself. Aleksandr Todorsky, an army officer before his arrest, was made Lt. General and deployed in the exoneration of Stalin's thousands of military victims.[3] Other rehabilitated Gulag survivors, as we saw earlier, were appointed members of the commissions sent in 1956 to liberate people still in the camps.

Shatunovskaya and Snegov were the most influential and, as one writer characterized Shatunovskaya, "indomitable." Both lived long lives—Snegov died in 1989, Shatunovskaya a year later—but they remain little-known figures. Snegov is known mainly from oral accounts and a few fragmentary memoirs and archive documents.[4] There is more information about Shatunovskaya. During the Gorbachev years, she reemerged to tell part of her story. After her death, her family published memoirs she had secretly taped, and a close friend, Grigory Pomerants, a non-conformist philosopher and fellow returnee, wrote a book about her. It presents the case, however biased in her favor, for Shatunovskaya as "one of the most remarkable women" in Russian political history.[5]

In private discussions and written communications, Shatunovskaya and Snegov "opened the eyes" of Khrushchev and Mikoyan, as the sons of both leaders later confirmed, to the full dimensions and horrors of the terror.[6] It was these two former zeks now at his side who persuaded the new Party leader to order the immediate release of all the victims in exile, and who then helped convince Khrushchev to deliver his historic anti-Stalin speech at the 1956 Party congress. And in the aftermath, again insisting that "otherwise the people will die," Shatunovskaya and Snegov persuaded Khrushchev and Mikoyan to send the "unloading" commissions directly to the camps.[7]

It was only the beginning of their role. As opposition to these and other de-Stalinizing measures intensified in ruling circles, Khrushchev and Mikoyan "needed" Shatunovskaya and Snegov as their "eyes and ears"[8]—and also, it seems, for their souls. All of Stalin's heirs, as I already explained, had been responsible for thousands of deaths during the terror-years, but only Khrushchev and Mikoyan became repentant Stalinists. (I came across no evidence that any of the others—Molotov, Kaganovich, Voroshilov, or Malenkov—took any initiatives to help survivors after Stalin's death, except, of course, Molotov in the release of his own wife.)

Mikoyan, a small, heavily mustached, and reportedly sympathetic Armenian, is usually remembered for having served with every Soviet leader from Lenin to Brezhnev, but his efforts on behalf of terror victims after Stalin's death was also remarkable. As a senior member of the new leadership, Mikoyan supported, even spurred, Khrushchev's anti-Stalinist initiatives while undertaking several of his own. During the open sessions of the 1956 Party congress, before Khrushchev's speech, for example, Mikoyan was the only speaker to mention by name, and thereby exonerate, several prominent victims, including Vladimir Antonov-

Ovseyenko, Anton's father; and he chaired the first commission on rehabilitation, before it became general policy, as well as one overseeing the return of several deported nationalities.

Privately, Mikoyan was even more active, personally intervening on behalf of many victims, sometimes on his own initiative, apparently with little regard to their political backgrounds. Among them were the former Stalinist official Milchakov, but also children of the leading anti-Stalinist oppositionists, Bukharin and Rykov; Bulat Okudzhava and his returnee mother, whom Mikoyan had known in the past, as well as the young Yelena Bonner, Sakharov's future wife; and survivors of the more recent Leningrad terror in which Malenkov, still a powerful member of the leadership, had been deeply complicit.[9]

That Mikoyan sometimes met personally with relatives of victims in whose arrest he himself had been complicit—one was Bukharin's son, Yuri Larin—suggested a need for absolution. The same seemed true of his close relationship with the uncompromising Shatunovskaya. One of Mikoyan's interventions particularly impressed returnees. An elderly zek, Mikhail Yakubovich, had been left destitute and homeless after his release. Unable to have him rehabilitated in Moscow, as he had done for others, because Yakubovich had been a member of an anti-Leninist party in 1917, Mikoyan arranged a pension and residence for him in Soviet Kazakhstan. Such deeds convinced some insiders that Mikoyan was the former Stalinist "most distraught by his conscience."[10]

Whatever their degrees of repentance, Mikoyan could have done little had Khrushchev not played his much larger role. It is usually assumed that Khrushchev's anti-Stalinism was entirely self-serving, merely a tactic he adopted for his struggle against Stalin's other heirs. It is true that he used the Stalin issue, sometimes inconsistently and selectively, in his drive for supreme power. But that factor alone cannot explain why he made anti-Stalinism such a large and recurring part of his decade-long leadership. Nor does suffering in his own family. "Only" as Khrushchev put it, his daughter-in-law ended up in the Gulag. (Certainly, Molotov was baffled by the apparent turnabout in his nemesis: "I thought he would be the same person he was before.")[11]

Indeed, politics cannot explain the personal risks Khrushchev took by exposing official crimes or his extraordinary initiatives in freeing and helping the survivors. The power struggle did not require, for example, publicizing so many details about those atrocities; appointing former zeks to positions of authority, even ones he had victimized; empowering young prosecutors like Ryazhsky to overturn falsified cases; placing children of victims, like Leonid Petrovsky and Pyotr Yakir, at prestigious academic institutions; or shielding others, like the writer Vasily Aksyonov, when they were threatened by his own men. Indeed, Khrushchev expended more political capital on his anti-Stalinism than he acquired, as in 1961 when he imposed on the Party elite his decision to publish Solzhenitsyn's novel about the camps, *One Day in the Life of Ivan Denisovich*.[12]

The best biography of Khrushchev calls his 1956 speech exposing Stalin's crimes "the bravest and most reckless thing he ever did," and asks, "Was he seeking to buttress his power or to assuage what was left of his conscience?" In private, Khrushchev spoke frequently about his conscience. Having heard the "voices of comrades who perished," he hoped that "people who have committed crimes . . . can admit it, and when they do so, it will bring them leniency if not exculpation." More explicitly, he told Mikhail Shatrov, "I have blood on my hands up to my elbows . . . This is the most terrible thing that burdens my soul." Years after he fell from power, he was still hoping "to die an honorable person."[13]

Terror victims who knew Khrushchev or who wanted to understand him—Solzhenitsyn, Yakir, Shatunovskaya, Antonov-Ovseyenko, Medvedev, Aikhenvald, Kopelev, Shatrov, Anna Larina, and others—concluded that his decision to expose the mass crimes of the Stalin era could be explained only by a "movement of the heart." Many also believed that his moral awakening had been influenced by "Khrushchev's zeks." (Pomerants thought Shatunovskaya had become Khrushchev's "gray bishop.") How else to explain, they pointed out, his astonishing proposal, at a Party congress broadcast to the entire nation in 1961, to build a national memorial to Stalin's victims—one that remains unbuilt even today?[14]

Exposing those crimes, along with the complicity of several leaders still on the scene, brought Khrushchev into repeated conflicts with powerful opponents during his ten years in office. In almost every major episode, his zeks continued to play a role. When Khrushchev initiated trials of the secret police boss, Lavrenti Beria, and other Stalinist "hangmen," from 1953 to 1955, Gulag survivors appeared as witnesses. Most were aged, unknown, or long-forgotten victims, but when Beria saw Snegov, whom he had known before having him arrested in 1939, he was stunned: "You're still alive!"[15]

Three years later, when Khrushchev secretly prepared his political bomb for the 1956 Party congress, again assisted (and prodded) by Snegov, he made sure that a number of other freed Communist zeks were invited and visible to the 1400 delegates in the hall. The sudden reappearance of those long-missing, barely alive comrades created, a delegate told me thirty years later, an audible "shock" in the corridors. And the following year, when Khrushchev struck back at the leading unrepentant Stalinists now trying to overthrow him—Molotov, Kaganovich, Malenkov, and Voroshilov—Shatunovskaya and Snegov provided him with documents proving the personal complicity of his enemies in Stalin's crimes.

On two subsequent occasions, Khrushchev relied on making the voices of survivors public. In October 1961, he decided to strike openly at the tenacious cult of Stalin as a great leader by removing the despot's body from the Lenin Mausoleum on Red Square, where it had lain since 1953. To provoke a seemingly spontaneous resolution at the Party congress that month, he arranged for another elderly Communist returnee and friend of Lenin, Dora Lazurkina, to tell the delegates, "Yesterday, I sought the advice of Ilich [Lenin], and it seemed as though he stood before me alive and said, 'I do not like being alongside Stalin, who inflicted so much grief on the Party.'" Stalin's body was removed that night. (Molotov never forgave Lazurkina, years later cursing her as "a sheer witch.")[16]

To substantiate his revelations about the mass terror, and to defend the release of millions of victims, Khrushchev also needed to explode the myth of Stalin's Gulag as "correctional labor." He did so by authorizing publication, in 1962, of another unknown zek's account of the camps, Solzhenitsyn's *One Day in the Life of Ivan Denisovich*. The novel's unvarnished portrayal, punctuated with zek language and rendered by a master writer, made clear the Gulag's brutality and the innocence of its political victims. Returnees I knew later recalled their reaction to the novel's sensational appearance. "At last," they thought, "the truth is out, and it can never again be denied." They were only half-right.

By the 1960s, returnees were contributing to de-Stalinization in another important way. Controversy over the past often inflames politics, but rarely so intensely as in the Soviet 1950s and 1960s, when the Stalin era was still "living history" for most Soviet adults. Their understanding of it had been shaped by decades of personal sacrifice and a falsified official history maintained by censorship and repression. According to that official version, Stalin's rule was a succession of great national achievements, from collectivization and industrialization in the 1930s to the nation's victory over Nazi Germany in 1945 and rise to superpower status. Post-Stalin elites were a product of that era, and for them it legitimized their power and privileges. As a young writer (and victim's son), Yuri Trifonov, soon discovered, they were determined to "defend it, defending themselves."[17]

But "the scale on which the dead have come back to life," as even Stalin's daughter observed from her lofty perspective, was irrefutable evidence of a parallel history of equally great crimes. Many returnees remained silent, but many others did not. As Khrushchev had foreseen, they told "relatives and friends and acquaintances what really happened." At Moscow's Institute of History alone, about a dozen victims returned and spoke candidly about their experiences. For young people in particular, "Their testimonies shed new light on events."[18]

In the 1950s and 1960s, most of the returnees who spoke out were still pro-Soviet, blaming mainly Stalin for their misfortunes. Their loyalist accounts of the past contributed to the revised history Khrushchev needed for his politics of reform. But other long-repressed traditions were also represented. Yakubovich and Irina Kakhovskaya, another survivor freed in her seventies, wanted justice for their slain moderate Marxist and pro-peasant comrades of 1917. Solzhenitsyn, Father Dudko, and Gumilyov spoke for Russia's older religious and nationalist values. My friend Mikhail Baitalsky wanted to redeem his Trotskyist comrades but also his own Jewish origins.

Like Holocaust survivors, Stalinist victims wrote memoirs, even though they conflicted with sanctioned history, because "This Must Not Happen Again," as Suren Gazaryan titled his. Anna Larina, for instance, began writing her memoirs in the 1960s, working secretly for years until chapters were ready to give to me for safe-keeping in the late 1970s. Several of these essential twentieth-century testimonies, such as Gnedin's *Catastrophe and Rebirth*, still have not been translated, but others are available in English: Larina's *This I Cannot Forget*, Ginzburg's *Journey Into the Whirlwind* and *Within the Whirlwind*, Kopelev's three volumes mentioned earlier, Razgon's *True Stories*, and Baitalsky's *Notebooks for the Grandchildren*.

For these older survivors, telling the still-forbidden full truth about the Stalin-era was, in the words of Antonov-Ovseyenko, "a duty to those who died at his hands, to those who survived that dark night, to those who will come after us."[19] (Solzhenitsyn's *The Gulag Archipelago* was, of course, the monumental product of this commitment.) Younger children of Stalin's victims, however, faced a difficult decision about their futures in the Soviet system. (Aksyonov and Bonner were advised by their mothers to attend medical school because it was "easier for doctors to survive in the camps," and they took the advice.) With their adult lives ahead of them, most put the past aside and chose political conformity. For them, "family and work became prized achievements."[20] In the 1960s and 1970s, Svyatoslav Fyodorov, to take a famous example, whose father returned after seventeen years in the Gulag, pioneered revolutionary eye surgeries to treat cataracts, glaucoma, and myopia.

Indeed, many children of victims went on to successful careers in the state and Party bureaucracies. In the early 1960s, a novelist researching the Stalinist terror in Siberia met the son of deported peasant parents who had died in those harsh circumstances. The young man had remained in Siberia, and now was head of a district Young Communist organization and awaiting promotion to an important Party position in Moscow. His brother and sister were also moving up the Soviet career ladder. None of them "bore any grudge against the authorities."[21]

The "phenomenon of Pyotr Masherov," whose father died in the Gulag in 1938, was more remarkable. From 1965 until his death in an accident in 1980, Masherov, as head of the Belorussian Communist Party and a candidate member of the national Politburo, was part of the small elite that ruled the Soviet Union. In this case too we are told not to be surprised that "the son of a person illegally repressed by the Soviet authorities (and rehabilitated in 1959) could be a sincere, convinced supporter of that same regime . . . Such were the times, and the people, forged in the crucible of the 1930s and 1940s."[22]

But other children of victims followed the lead of outspoken older returnees. The Medvedev brothers and Antonov-Ovseyenko had already begun collecting materials for their histories of the Stalin era. Trifonov, Leonid Petrovsky, Yuri Gastyev, Pyotr Yakir, and Kamil Ikramov were preparing biographies of their martyred fathers. (Most did so out of filial duty, though Gastyev began when a senior prosecutor told him it was the best way to have his father rehabilitated.) Meanwhile, a group of children of executed generals was gathering documents "restoring historical truth" for museums and schools in provincial cities.[23]

Only a small portion of this historical truth-telling could be published in the Soviet Union during and shortly after Khrushchev's Thaw. But enough became known, along with increasingly explicit literary accounts, and not only Solzhenitsyn's, to frighten officials throughout the system. It revealed that their power and privileges had also resulted from the victimization of millions of their fellow citizens. Not surprisingly, they were "afraid of History."[24]

Anti-Stalinism both enhanced and endangered Khrushchev's leadership. Exposing official crimes gave his other policies a moral dimension and helped spur progressive changes. The social needs of returnees, for example, contributed to important welfare and legal reforms. His leadership also inspired a new, reform-minded generation of Soviet intellectuals and officials. Some, like the prosecutor Ryazhsky, had an immediate impact. (Nikolai Vavilov's son remained so grateful to the prosecutor who rehabilitated his father that many years later he sought him out, only to discover the now aged man had lost his memory.)[25] Others, who came to be known as the "people of the 1960s" and thought of themselves as "children of Khrushchev's Twentieth Party Congress," gradually moved up through the system. Thirty years later, led by Mikhail Gorbachev, their turn came.

But Khrushchev's revelations also galvanized powerful opposition against him. The crimes of the past threatened not only Stalin's personal cohorts like Molotov, Kaganovich, Voroshilov, and Malenkov, who had signed his lists condemning thousands of innocent people, but a legion of lesser figures with bloodstains on their careers. Two of them were close to Khrushchev's own ruling circle—General Ivan Serov, the first head of the post-Stalin KGB, who had been deeply involved in the wartime deportations and later in an infamous torture-prison, and Mikhail Suslov, a rising Party ideologist who became one of the most powerful and reactionary political oligarchs of the Brezhnev era.

Their attempts to sabotage Khrushchev's returnee policies are vividly recalled in Shatunovskaya's memoirs.[26] When he and Mikoyan ordered the release of victims in exile, Malenkov and Suslov derailed the instructions until Shatunovskaya informed Mikoyan, who alerted Khrushchev. Malenkov, Suslov, and others then tried to rig the composition of the commissions being sent to free Gulag inmates. His opponents hated all of Khrushchev's zeks now "in fashion," particularly Shatunovskaya, who used her position at Party headquarters not merely to process rehabilitation applications but to actively solicit them. Serov's agents followed her, intercepted her mail, tapped her phones, and tried "to isolate" her because of her "very bad influence on Khrushchev." And when Khrushchev made Shatunovskaya the lead investigator of Stalin-era crimes, empowering her to interrogate Molotov, Kaganovich, and others, they protested bitterly against letting "ex-convicts judge us."[27]

The neo-Stalinists, as they now were, fought back. Khrushchev appointed Serov, a longtime NKVD general and personal crony, to head the new KGB, but had to replace him.

Molotov, Kaganovich, and Voroshilov attempted a classic cover-up, chairing a commission to investigate criminal events in which they were personally involved. When that failed, they tried to neuter Khrushchev's 1956 speech and then blunt its consequences. Meanwhile, their agents scoured secret police and Party archives for documents demonstrating Khrushchev's own role in the terror, while destroying materials that incriminated them. (Khrushchev's representatives were, of course, doing the same on his behalf.)[28] And when that threat did not deter him, they moved in 1957 to depose him, nearly succeeding.

Their fear of a "judgment day" was well-founded.[29] As conflicts over the past intensified, questions began to emerge about high-level criminal responsibility similar to the charges formalized at the Nuremberg Trial in Germany a decade before. The analogy was hard to ignore. The Soviet Union had been one of the governments prosecuting those crimes against humanity. (Indeed, Khrushchev's new Procurator-General, Roman Rudenko, had been the lead Soviet prosecutor.) And with so many Gulag survivors now visible in the Soviet Union and their experiences increasingly known, the Holocaust-like dimensions of Stalin-era "repressions" were becoming clear.

When Stalin's other successors put on trial and executed "Beria's gang" in 1953, 1954, and 1955, they attempted to obscure any larger implications. The proceedings were closed, Beria was falsely convicted of treason and espionage, and his misdeeds were disassociated from Stalin's remaining heirs. Even so, the charge of "crimes against humanity" was made in at least one case, and the presence of Gulag survivors as witnesses was clear evidence of the real crimes. Reactions to Khrushchev's revelations at the 1956 Party congress indicated that such issues were already just below the surface. Questions were asked at lower-level Party meetings and elsewhere (and quickly suppressed) about the entire leadership's responsibility, including Khrushchev's, for what had happened.[30]

Nonetheless, he soon crossed another rubicon, though again behind closed doors. In June 1957, at a meeting of the full Central Committee, Khrushchev and his supporters staged a kind of trial of Molotov, Kaganovich, and Malenkov.[31] Quoting horrific documents unearthed by Shatunovskaya and others, they accused Molotov and Kaganovich, along with Stalin, of having been responsible for more than 1.5 million arrests in 1937 and 1938 alone and personally sanctioning 38,679 executions during that period, 3,167 on one day. Bloodthirsty orders in their handwriting were read aloud to the assembled Party elite: "Beat, beat, and beat again . . .Scoundrel, scum . . .only one punishment—death."

A Soviet Nuremberg seemed to be looming. When the accused defended their actions as "mistakes," they were met with shouts of "No, crimes!" A Khrushchev supporter hurled a threat at the three senior Stalinist leaders that must have chilled other longtime bosses in the hall: "If the people knew that their hands are dripping with innocent blood, they would greet them not with applause but stones." It was too much for one Central Committee member, until then a Khrushchev supporter, who "profoundly" objected to the suggestion that "people who headed and led our Party for so many years turn out to be murderers who now must be put in the dock."[32] In the end, however, Molotov, Kaganovich, and Malenkov were only expelled from the leadership and Central Committee and banished to minor posts far from Moscow.

It was a moment of high drama, but the crimes still greatly exceeded the punishment. In the early and mid-1950s, some fifty to one hundred secret police bosses and brutal interrogators—one could not remember whether or not he had tortured Aleksandr Todorsky—were tried and sentenced; between twenty-five and thirty were sentenced to death, and the rest were sent to prison. (Exact numbers still have not been made known.) Another 2,370 were reported to have been fired or subjected to administrative sanctions, from loss of their ranks, awards, and Party membership to their pensions. In all, between 1954 and 1963, approximately 46,000 KGB officers were dismissed, though not all of them for abuses committed during the terror.[33]

In addition, in the aftermath of Khrushchev's revelations, a dozen or so NKVD generals and Gulag camp commandants committed suicide, most by pistol shot, a few by opening their veins in a bathtub. (Many years later, such a scene was portrayed, though misdated, in the Oscar-winning Russian film, *Burnt by the Sun*.) But it was the suicide of Stalin's former literary overlord, Aleksandr Fadeyev, that most unnerved the political establishment.[34] A civilian and a cultured man, Fadeyev had not, after all, personally tortured or executed anyone, only acquiesced in the arrest of his colleagues, as had so many other members of the Stalinist elite.

Khrushchev's zeks regarded those episodes of justice as only first steps and implored him to punish all of those guilty, even to put Stalin's entire regime on public trial. Khrushchev resisted such "a St Bartholomew's Eve massacre," as he remarked, no doubt for several reasons. How, it was being asked, to judge degrees of complicity in two decades of mass terror? Roy Medvedev argued that it depended on "what a person could have done to prevent crimes." But what about the "honest" and "kind" NKVD men remembered by Serebryakova, Ikramov, and Razgon? Or the lowly Gulag guards, a "rag-tag collection of poorly educated and poorly paid unfortunates"? Or the stepfather of my Moscow publisher, an ordinary soldier ordered to participate in the lethal deportation of the Chechen people?[35]

By some reckonings, the mass terror had been possible only due to mass guilt. An estimated five percent of the nation had been secret informers and at least one million people had been Gulag camp employees, including economic managers and bookkeepers. Indeed, a remorseful poet who had prospered under Stalin now concluded that everyone who had remained silent "bears responsibility for the blood of Lubyanka, the hell of interrogations." (Shatunovskaya had a copy of the unpublished poem.) Such thinking meant, Khrushchev objected, "More people would have to be imprisoned than had been rehabilitated and released."[36]

He also had, of course, an intensely personal reason for not going too far. "Hangmen" now on trial or committing suicide insisted they had "only obeyed orders" of higher Stalinist authorities and pointed to members of the current political leadership. Meanwhile, Khrushchev's enemies were circulating materials documenting that the "blood on his hands," as his admirer Gorbachev later learned, involved signing orders to arrest many innocent people.[37] For Khrushchev to make more charges of Stalin-era crimes, or more public ones, would mean endangering himself even more.

And yet, at the Twenty-Second Party Congress in October 1961, Khrushchev unleashed his most ramifying assault on the Stalinist past and its many defenders. He and his supporters considerably expanded the revelations and accusations made in 1956 and 1957—and now did so publicly. For the first time, daily newspaper and radio reports of the proceedings informed the nation of "monstrous crimes" and the need for "historical justice," along with lurid accounts of mass arrests, torture, and murder carried out under Stalin. For emphasis, Khrushchev's men reminded the country that the terror had struck "not only officials themselves but their families, even absolutely innocent children, whose lives, as a result, were shattered from the very beginning." The impact of the new revelations on the public was profound. The former zek Solzhenitsyn, whose novels about those events were not yet published, was astonished: "I don't remember reading anything as interesting as the speeches at the XXII Congress in a long time!"[38]

There was more. This time Khrushchev did not limit the indictment to crimes against Communist Party members, as he had done on previous occasions. The resolution removing Stalin's body from the Lenin Mausoleum spoke simply of "mass repressions against honest Soviet people." And for the first time, Khrushchev and his allies publicly accused Molotov, Kaganovich, and Malenkov of "direct personal responsibility" for those "illegal" acts and demanded they be expelled from the Party (as soon happened), which strongly suggested they might be put on trial. The specter of trials, inflated by Khrushchev's references to "numerous documents in our possession" and his call for a "comprehensive study of all such cases arising out of the abuse of power," sent tremors of fear through the thousands who also bore "direct personal responsibility."

The congress was a victory for Khrushchev's zeks. The radicalized anti-Stalinism unfurled at the most authoritative political forum was due in significant measure to their influence on Khrushchev and, it was revealed years later, to an important development behind the scenes. Prior to the congress, Khrushchev had established a high-level Party commission to carry out, as he hinted at the gathering, a "comprehensive study" of the darkest events of the Stalinist 1930s. The investigation focused on the 1934 assassination of the Party boss of Leningrad, Sergei Kirov, which had ignited the Great Terror, and on the subsequent public trials and execution of Bukharin and other founders of the Soviet Union.

Shatunovskaya was the commission's lead investigator. Mistrustful of the staff at Party headquarters, she recruited other Gulag returnees to assist her. (Milchakov was especially happy to be recalled to duty.) Sixty-four classified folders of evidence resulted from their findings in secret archives and from interviews with witnesses still alive. The commission concluded that Stalin had plotted those fateful events in order to launch the terror that consolidated his personal dictatorship and transformed the Soviet political system into a police state. On the eve of the congress, Shatunovskaya gave Khrushchev a summary of the findings. When he read it, she said, "he wept."[39]

———ɷ———

Khrushchev's initiatives at the 1961 Party congress unleashed a three-year struggle, in the Soviet establishment and in society, between the "friends and foes" of de-Stalinization.[40] Eased censorship enabled historians to begin criticizing the entire Stalin era, even his long sacrosanct collectivization of the peasantry and his conduct of the war, particularly the nation's un-preparedness for the German invasion in 1941 and the staggering costs—26.5 million dead—of victory in 1945. Revelations about forced collectivization cast doubt on a foundation of the existing political and economic system while those about the war challenged rationalizations underpinning the post-Stalin regime's domestic and foreign policies.

The growing number of literary depictions of the terror had an even greater impact. In 1962, reactions to Solzhenitsyn's *One Day in the Life of Ivan Denisovich* immediately became a litmus test of people's attitudes toward the Stalinist past, but other writers and editors were also seizing the moment to publish novels, short stories, plays, and poems on related subjects. In particular, the Gulag returnee now became a familiar figure in fiction with titles like *The Return of Dyuzhev* and *The Return of Yuri Metrofanovich*. Some of the best-known authors, including Kamil Ikramov and Vasily Aksyonov, had themselves been victims of the terror.[41]

Recurring themes in this thinly disguised fiction could only alarm members of the Soviet establishment who had made their careers under Stalin. One theme involved dark portrayals of officials and other prominent citizens who feared the return of the victims and thwarted their reintegration into society. Another was a generational conflict featuring sons who asked their fathers searing questions about why they had not helped doomed relatives and friends. Above all, there was the looming question of responsibility for the millions of victims who would never return, as suggested in this poem by Lez Ozerov:

The dead speak. Without periods.
And without commas. Almost without words.
From concentration camps. From isolation cells.
From houses savagely burning.

The dead speak. Notebooks.
Letters. Testaments. Diaries.
Signature of a hasty hand
On the rough surface of bricks.

With a piece of iron on the frozen cot.
On the wall with a fragment of broken glass.
Life, while it lasted, left its signature
On the prison floor in a tricklet of blood.[42]

Such publications were, as Suslov later complained bitterly, the result of Khrushchev's political initiatives. So were suddenly revived hopes—and fears—that Stalin-era crimes would be more fully punished. In 1956, a former zek on the commissions sent to liberate the Gulag had asked Shatunovskaya, "When will these criminals, who for years destroyed innocent Soviet people, be brought to justice?" The prospect of new trials had been raised in 1957, but only behind closed doors and in passing. Hence the extraordinary impact of public statements at the 1961 Party congress about people complicit in the crimes, including this remark by a close Khrushchev associate: "They should be haunted by nightmares. They should hear the sobbing and curses of the mothers, wives, and children of the innocent comrades who perished."[43]

Emboldened by statements at the top, and by the renewed prospect of leading Stalinists being put on trial, a growing number of returnees began pursuing others who bore "personal responsibility" for their misfortunes. (Eugenia Ginzburg said of one, "It is written on his face.")[44] Some of their demands were symbolic. Inspired by Khrushchev's order to strip cities of Stalin's name and dismantle monuments in his honor, petitions were circulated demanding that the ashes of the show-trial prosecutor Vyshinsky be removed from his honored place in the Kremlin Wall and the remains of the executioner-judge Ulrikh, who died in 1951, from Moscow's hallowed Novodevichy Cemetery.

Most of the calls for justice, however, pointed to accomplices still active in virtually every Soviet profession. Three cases became widely known in Moscow, one of special interest to surviving children of the original Leninist guard. Andrei Sverdlov, the son of another Soviet founder, had been their childhood friend and schoolmate. When he later appeared in their prison cells as a NKVD interrogator, as in Anna Larina's, they were shocked and further demoralized. Known for his "pathological cruelty," Sverdlov personally tortured several of his former playmates. By the early 1960s, while still a colonel in the secret police, he was making a new career as a scholar and author of detective stories for children.[45] The friends Sverdlov had betrayed began a campaign to have him exposed and punished.

In another realm savaged by the terror, several highly placed literary critics were known to have been informers for the NKVD, regularly writing letters denouncing the political views of their colleagues. Members of the cultural community now wanted them exposed and punished, scrawling on the prestigious dacha of one, "Beware—An Evil Dog!" Yakov Elsberg, a critic who had been involved in the arrest and death of a number of novelists and poets, was the target of a particularly determined campaign that succeeded in having him expelled, at least temporarily, from the Writers Union and the Communist Party.[46]

More threatening to complicit officials in high political places was the campaign initiated by a returnee, Pavel Shabalkin, to bring two leading Stalinist philosophers, Pavel Yudin and Mark Mitin, to justice. Both had contributed to the death of colleagues and to Shabalkin's long imprisonment, and had then plagiarized their work. Yudin and Mitin were not, however, merely philosophers. Until recently, they had been important political functionaries, members of the Party's Central Committee, and Yudin even a candidate member of the Politburo. Like Sverdlov and Elsberg, Yudin and Mitin escaped real punishment—both were appointed to a commission to draft a new Party program—and all four eventually died in official honor. But the campaigns against them were enough to cause panic and "mental breakdowns" among no less guilty people still in power.[47]

Ineluctably, it seemed, Nuremberg-like issues of collective guilt now began to appear, however guardedly and indirectly, in the officially sanctioned Soviet press. They were barely below the surface in the many sharply conflicting reviews of Solzhenitsyn and other publications about the terror, which, a cultural official angrily complained, "needlessly hasten to drag literary corpses out into the light." Some accusations were directed at the secret police, as in a novel whose hero, a young prosecutor not unlike Ryazhsky, tells a former NKVD major, "You will still pay for the years 1937 and 1938."[48] But other allegations directly threatened political functionaries still in office. In 1963, one occasion involving the venerable writer Ilya Ehrenburg, and entangling even Khrushchev, provoked an angry reaction by the political and literary establishment.

Unlike many prominent figures during the Stalin years, Ehrenburg had behaved honorably, avoiding direct complicity in the terror and demonstrating a "readiness to do good," even though his own life was in danger more than once. After Stalin's death, Ehrenburg helped returnees and other victims in various ways. He contributed to rehabilitations, as we saw in Meyerhold's case; he chose a former zek, Natalya Stolyarova, to be his personal secretary; he met with the widow and son of Bukharin, his boyhood friend; and he counseled children of other victims he had known. One, Vasily Aksyonov, asked him, "How did you manage to survive? It's very important for me to know." Ehrenburg replied, "I don't know."[49]

But, of course, he did know, at least in part. In a chapter of his heavily censored memoirs published in 1963, Ehrenburg alluded to the reason, admitting it had been necessary for him "to live with clenched teeth" under Stalin because he knew his arrested friends and colleagues were innocent. Ehrenburg's confession, or "theory of a conspiracy of silence," as it became known, triggered a storm of furious attacks on him. It is easy to understand why: If the marginalized writer Ehrenburg had known the truth, so must have the multitude of Party and state officials above him. That meant, as one angrily protested, they all "were merely saving their own skins and thereby helping the evil to grow stronger."[50]

Still worse in their view, the early 1960s brought a spate of Soviet writings about Germany under Hitler. Much of this commentary was by inference clearly about the Soviet system under Stalin. Readers instinctively saw their own recent experiences in depictions of the Hitler cult, Gestapo, Nazi concentration camps, and widespread German complicity. When the powerful American film *Judgment at Nuremberg* was shown in Moscow in 1963, reactions were even more pointed. In light of that analogy, graphic accounts of Stalin's terror, and mounting calls for justice, "fears of being made to answer for their crimes" understandably spread through Soviet officialdom.[51]

At some point, even the younger men Khrushchev had put on his leadership council decided that his anti-Stalin initiatives were endangering too many people, perhaps the Soviet system itself. Unlike Suslov, Leonid Brezhnev and others who would rule the Soviet Union for the next twenty years had little or no blood on their hands, but plenty on their feet. Having risen so rapidly under Stalin as their predecessors were being swept away

by the terror, they had, as I often heard, a "complex about the past."
Their generational unease explains in part why, after deposing
Khrushchev in 1964, they reimposed strict censorship of the entire
Stalin era.

From the beginning, according to Khrushchev's son, his
father's anti-Stalinist policies had "practically isolated" him in
the very Party and state institutions he headed.[52] Considering
Khrushchev's accomplishments during his ten years in office, his
son clearly exaggerated. But it is true that Khrushchev was always
a challenged leader, especially on the Stalin question. Even after
defeating Molotov, Kaganovich, Voroshilov, Malenkov, and Serov,
he repeatedly encountered strong opposition. In 1957, one of his
own leading supporters defected over the issue of putting senior
Stalinists "in the dock." And although Khrushchev seeded the idea
of removing Stalin's body from the Lenin Mausoleum in 1956, it
took him nearly six years to do so.

Nor were freed zeks and other victims nominally under
his protection immune from attack. Shatunovskaya continued
to be harassed and sabotaged at the Party's headquarters. False
information about Snegov and Vasily Aksyonov found its way
to Khrushchev's desk. A Moscow academic director warned my
friend Igor Pyatnitsky that unless he conformed, he would "end
up like your father." Despite Khrushchev's backing in 1963 and
1964, Solzhenitsyn was denied the Lenin Prize for literature for
One Day in the Life of Ivan Denisovich. Meanwhile, the Party boss
of Leningrad refused to rehabilitate or give pensions to victims
returning to his city.[53]

Outwardly, the 1961 Party congress had seemed to be a
major victory for anti-Stalinism and for Khrushchev personally.
In reality, most of the new leaders he had promoted disregarded
their benefactor's initiatives, remaining conspicuously silent about
the crimes of the past. Some high-ranking delegates who did echo
Khrushchev's anti-Stalinist line were actually "against all of it."

Even the decision to remove Stalin's body, complained one of the men who plotted Khrushchev's overthrow, had been "taken by a narrow circle of leaders."[54]

Indeed, opposition to Khrushchev's anti-Stalinism grew stronger after the congress, no doubt in response to it. That was the message of an alarmed poem by Yevgeny Yevtushenko, "The Heirs of Stalin," published on Khrushchev's instructions in the Party's flagship newspaper, *Pravda*, in October 1962. Several lines read like a dire warning, or a desperate plea for help:

> We removed him from the Mausoleum.
> But how to remove Stalin's heirs from Stalin?!

> Some of his heirs tend roses in retirement,
> but secretly think their retirement is temporary.
> Others even curse Stalin from tribunes,
> but at night yearn for the old times.

> They who once supported him,
> don't like these times of emptied camps.[55]

Behind the scenes, Khrushchev was being defeated or forced to retreat. He felt surrounded by opponents who "were shooting me in the back with their eyes."[56] In 1962, Shatunovskaya and Snegov were driven from their official positions. Both complained that Khrushchev had let them down by yielding to neo-Stalinists and failing to rely on younger, anti-Stalinist forces in the Communist Party apparatus. Perhaps that was true. Perhaps Khrushchev had grown frightened of his own initiatives or, approaching his seventieth birthday, too old to fight. But it is not clear where he would have found new anti-Stalinists in the Party. Their time, and power, was still twenty years in the future.

Whatever the full explanation, more political setbacks followed. By 1963, rehabilitations had all but ended. Shatunovskaya's report on Stalinist crimes went unpublished and the materials she had collected were buried deep in a Party archive. (Even the executive summary was published only forty years later, and many of the materials disappeared.) In 1964, in addition to Solzhenitsyn's defeat in the campaign for the Lenin Prize, a major editorial authorized by Khrushchev on "Stalin and His Heirs" was aborted. So too were constitutional changes and reforms in the KGB he and Mikoyan proposed to prevent a recurrence of past abuses.[57] Meanwhile, nothing more was heard of his 1961 proposal to build a memorial to Stalin's victims.

When the Central Committee of the Communist Party overthrew Khrushchev behind closed doors in October 1964, neither the lengthy indictment presented there nor the public announcement mentioned the Stalin question. Both focused instead on the aging Khrushchev's failed economic and foreign policies (most recently, the Cuban Missile Crisis in 1962), perpetual reorganization of governing institutions, increasingly capricious behavior, and dismissive attitude toward "collective leadership."[58] There was considerable truth in all of those charges.

But Khrushchev's anti-Stalinist approach to the past and the present was a central, even if scarcely mentioned, cause of his overthrow. It was, after all, the driving force behind his decade-long attempt to reform the Soviet system, which was now being ended by a sharp conservative backlash. One expression of that backlash was the upsurge of pro-Stalinist sentiments among high-level Party and state officials, who were now privately complaining that "thousands of wreckers could not have done as much harm to the country in decades as Nikita [Khrushchev] has done."[59]

Khrushchev may have retreated, but in the months leading to his ouster he showed no sign of abandoning anti-Stalinism. In January, the government newspaper, edited by Khrushchev's son-in-law, gave unusual attention to a current provincial official who had adopted Stalin's "criminal and malicious" methods. When a powerful Party oligarch protested recent publications Khrushchev had authorized, the aging leader defiantly replied, "If the poem of Yevtushenko and the novel of Solzhenitsyn are anti-Soviet, then I am also anti-Soviet." Nor could Khrushchev's opponents have felt safe when, barely three months before his overthrow, the same newspaper controlled by his son-in-law charged that when they entered the elite under Stalin, "False denunciations frequently became a ladder by which to climb to the top."[60]

Looking back, Solzhenitsyn rightly concluded that the well-organized campaign to deny him the 1964 Lenin Prize had been a "rehearsal for the 'putsch' against Nikita." When the transcript of that Central Committee meeting was finally published forty-three years later, there was more evidence. In secret discussions prior to the formal sessions, Khrushchev was accused of "reviling Stalin to the point of indecency." Suslov, who resented Khrushchev for having "supported all this camp literature,"[61] delivered the detailed indictment. Only Mikoyan tried to defend him.

Any doubts were soon dispelled when the new leadership began ending anti-Stalinist policies related to the past and restoring the tyrant's historical reputation. Certainly, people with vested interests understood the meaning of Khrushchev's ouster. Solzhenitsyn called it a "small October revolution" and began smuggling abroad his unpublished manuscripts about the terror. And while NKVD men imprisoned in the mid-1950s rejoiced, some former zeks worried, "They will now start arresting us."[62]

Left: Khrushchev giving his "secret" speech at the Twentieth Party Congress, February 1956, denouncing Stalin's crimes. (Credit: Novosti)

Below: Khrushchev, in forced retirement, with Mikhail Shatrov (far right, wearing eyeglasses) and other friends and family members. (Courtesy of Mikhail Shatrov)

List of "rehabilitated Old Bolsheviks" to be invited to the Twentieth Party Congress that Aleksei Snegov prepared for Khushchev, with the year each had joined the Party. Olga Shatunovskaya is listed third, Snegov fifth, and Aleksandr Milchakov twelfth.

Olga Shatunovskaya (seated far right) and Valentina Pikina (seated second from the left) with other members of the Communist Party Control Committee, 1958. (Shatunovskaya family archive)

Shatunovskaya (left), after her ouster from Communist Party headquarters, Anastas Mikoyan, and his wife, Ashkhen, 1963. (Shatunovskaya family archive)

Boris Ryazhsky, one of the young procurators empowered under Khrushchev to reopen cases and rehabilitate Stalin's victims. (Credit: *Teatralnaia zhizn*)

An example of the "sacred" document of rehabilitation issued to victims or their surviving relatives under Khrushchev, though this one, confirming Bukharin's "posthumous" exoneration, was issued to his widow Anna Larina only under Mikhail Gorbachev, in 1988.

СПРАВКА   КОПИЯ

Военная Коллегия
Верховного Суда
Союза ССР

09   февраля 19 88г.
№ СП-002/37

212160, Москва, ул Воронского, д. 15

Дело по обвинению Бухарина Николая Ивановича, до ареста 27 февраля 1937 г. - Главный редактор газеты "Известия", пересмотрено Пленумом Верховного Суда СССР 4 февраля 1988 года.

Приговор Военной коллегии Верховного Суда СССР от 13 марта 1938 года в отношении Бухарина Н.И. отменен и дело прекращено за отсутствием в его действиях состава преступления.

Бухарин Николай Иванович реабилитирован посмертно.

НАЧАЛЬНИК СЕКРЕТАРИАТА ВОЕННОЙ
КОЛЛЕГИИ ВЕРХОВНОГО СУДА СССР
ПОЛКОВНИК ЮСТИЦИИ

А.НИКОНОВ

The son and widow of Red Army Commander Yakir, Pyotr and Sarra, both longtime Gulag inmates, with Pyotr's daughter Irina, Moscow, early 1960s. (Courtesy of Alexandra Aikhenvald)

Vasily Aksyonov, Eugenia Ginzburg's son, and his father Pavel Aksyonov, who spent eighteen years in the Gulag, at Vasily's dacha near Moscow, 1980, on the eve of his emigration to the United States.

The author's (kneeling) first meeting with Bukharin's widow, Anna Larina, and son Yuri Larin, at Larina's Moscow apartment, August 1975.

Forefront, from left to right: Lynn Blair Cohen (then the author's wife); their children, Alexandra and Andrew; the author; Yuri Larin's son, Nikolai ("Kolya"); and Anna Larina's other son, Mikhail ("Misha") Fadeyev. Back row, left to right: Inge Ballod, Yuri's wife; Anna; and Yuri, late 1976.

Anna Larina with her grandchildren, Eka (left) and Kolya; and daughter Nadezhda ("Nadya") Fadeyeva, New Year's Eve, 1981.

Larina and her Gulag suitcase.

From the left: the author's son, Andrew; Anna Larina; Yevgeny Gnedin; the author; Yuri Larin; and Inge Ballod, late 1976.

The author with Roy Medvedev, at Roy's apartment, 1981.

And with Anton Antonov-Ovseyenko, at his apartment, 1980.

Tanya Bayeva, at her apartment, 1980; and Yuri Gastyev.

Tanya Bayeva and Katrina vanden Heuvel (the author's wife), at Tanya's apartment, mid-1980s.

Igor Pyatnitsky, mid-1980s.

Leonid Petrovsky with Yuri Larin; and Yevgeny Gnedin, early 1980s.

Khrushchev's gravesite at Moscow's Novodevichy Cemetery, the headstone designed by the sculptor Ernst Neizvestny to reflect the dark and bright chapters of Khrushchev's life.

CHAPTER 5

The Victims Vanish, and Return Again

The rehabilitated are no longer in fashion.
—A Communist Party official, 1967

We cannot and should not ever forgive or justify what happened.
—Mikhail Gorbachev, 1987

The saga of Gulag survivors and Stalin's other victims did not end with Khrushchev's overthrow, or even with the disappearance of the Soviet Union twenty-seven years later. Many things changed, but the precarious status of Stalin's victims, in Soviet and post-Soviet Russia, has continued to depend on his official reputation and, inseparably since 1964, on that of Khrushchev. Meanwhile, the official standing of those two historical figures has been determined by a still-larger factor—the relative strength of reformers and conservatives in the ruling class.[1]

Ever since Stalin's death in 1953, his legacy has profoundly divided Russia's elites and society alike. The dispute derives, as I pointed out before, from the dual nature of his long rule. Looking back on the Stalin years, many Russians still see towering national achievements, from the industrialization of a backward peasant country to the victory over Nazi Germany, while many others see equally towering crimes and millions of victims. Pro-Stalin opinion insists that his "mistakes" or "excesses" were fully justified by the historic accomplishments. Anti-Stalin opinion replies that nothing justifies such crimes and that the nation would have achieved more, at far less cost, without Stalin's horrific abuses of power.

This unresolved, polarizing controversy has been part of Russian intellectual and cultural life for almost sixty years, but its most important role has been in political struggles at the highest levels. Reformers, who have wanted to diminish or even dismantle the monopolistic state controls Stalin imposed on politics, economics, and society in the 1930s, have highlighted the criminality of that era in order to discredit the system that resulted from it and to legitimize their proposed changes. Conservatives, on the other hand, in arguing that many state controls should be maintained, have minimized, even covered up, the historical crimes.

Soviet political history after Stalin developed along those lines. Khrushchev's policies represented the first attempt to carry out fundamental reforms in the system inherited from Stalin. Hence his revelations about the terror and rehabilitation of many of its victims. The eighteen-year-reign of Khrushchev's successor, Leonid Brezhnev, from 1964 to 1982, emerged in reaction to those reforms and soon grew into, as a historian, and former zek, noted, "Russia's first truly conservative era since the Revolution."

Like conservatives elsewhere, the Brezhnev leadership needed a glorious past that sanctified the existing order. It therefore heeded the call, in the words of an ultra-conservative poet, to "put Stalin back on the pedestal."[2] In the long shadow that pedestal cast over the Stalin era, the crimes all but vanished, along with their victims. They reappeared only after 1985, with the rise of Mikhail Gorbachev and the radical anti-Stalinist reformation he called Perestroika.

—⟊⟊—

Gulag survivors who feared that Khrushchev's successors would have them re-arrested misunderstood the nature of the new regime, as have Western historians who characterize Brezhnev's policies as a "re-Stalinization" of the Soviet Union. The men who deposed Khrushchev represented the upper echelons of the vast Party-state administrative bureaucracy, or nomenklatura, which itself had been repeatedly victimized by Stalin's terror. They had no interest in restoring such a regime but in assuring it would never recur.

Indeed, the yearning of Soviet officials to be free of a terroristic personal dictatorship above them was the primary reason they initially supported Khrushchev's de-Stalinizing measures. After years of fearful survival, watching their superiors being swept away, they wanted to become a normal bureaucratic class with secure positions and futures for themselves and their families. By the early 1960s, with the terror ended, the Communist Party apparatus restored to political primacy, and the secret police under its control, they had largely gained what they wanted.

That yearning for security was also why Khrushchev's own elite turned against him. The revelations and populist attitudes engendered by his anti-Stalinist initiatives now seemed to threaten the ruling class in new ways. Anti-Stalinism had already sparked rebellions in the Soviet empire in Eastern Europe. By 1964, it was raising questions about the Soviet order at home, from collectivized agriculture to the one-party state, while breeding defiance of "all authority." Khrushchev's anti-Stalinism was also, ruling officials thought, "spitting on the history of our country," portraying their lives as "a chain of crimes and mistakes," and encouraging children to see only "fathers who were arrested and fathers who did the arresting."[3]

The Brezhnev leadership sought to end all of those de-stabilizing trends without resorting to anything approaching a new reign of terror. It managed to do so for two decades by embracing the post-Stalin status quo while reversing Khrushchev's anti-Stalinist "excesses," taming his other reforms, reimposing strict censorship, and practicing selective repression. The new regime's watch-words were those of conservatives everywhere: deference to authority, stability, reverence for the past, and as little change as possible in any direction, backward or forward. Lev Kopelev, one of the most insightful Gulag returnees, summarized the essence of the Brezhnev era in 1978: "We are ruled not by a Communist or a fascist party and not by a Stalinist party, but by a status quo party."[4]

Nonetheless, safeguarding a status quo whose institutions, administrative procedures, and ideological orthodoxies still derived from the Stalin era required the rehabilitation of the despot himself and his times, not his victims. As a high Brezhnev official instructed historians, "*All*—and I repeat, *all*—stages in the development of our Soviet society must be regarded as positive."[5] The exception was the stage featuring Khrushchev, who, apart from occasional references to "that adventurer," was deleted from official history.

By the end of the 1960s, Stalin was back on his pedestal as a historical leader. Serious criticism of his collectivization campaign and wartime leadership was banned; rehabilitations of his victims were ended; and intimations that there had ever been a great terror grew scant. Anti-Stalinism was condemned as an "anti-Communist slogan" invented in the West by enemies of the Soviet Union. Soviet citizens who criticized the Stalinist past much as Khrushchev had done at two Communist Party congresses could now be prosecuted for "slandering the Soviet social and state system." Once-honored anti-Stalinist writers and historians were persecuted or simply forbidden to publish. Their counterparts in official politics either conformed, were demoted, or had their careers terminated.

One political career that ended, to give a little-known but significant example, was that of Len Karpinsky, a rising young Party figure being groomed to be a future leader of the Soviet Union, whom I knew well years later. In the mid-1960s, Karpinsky, the son of Lenin's old friend who had helped Stalin's victims after their release, was already a national leader of the Young Communist organization and a top editor of the Party's directive-issuing newspaper, *Pravda*. He had been singled out for rapid promotion by members of the new Brezhnev regime, who told him, "We are pinning our hopes on you." Unwilling to abandon his anti-Stalinist convictions, including his outspoken support for Gulag returnees, Len was soon expelled from the Party and relegated to the life of an all-but unemployable outcast.[6]

In the months leading up to the ninetieth anniversary of Stalin's birth, on December 21, 1969, neo-Stalinists close to the Kremlin launched an aggressive campaign for the despot's unequivocal rehabilitation. A few political insiders, such as Len Karpinsky, and dissidents protested, as they had in the aftermath of Khrushchev's ouster, but with minimal success. The memorial article that appeared in the Party's leading newspaper, *Pravda*, professed to "balance" Stalin's "great contributions" and his "mistakes." Most importantly, however, it was the first official commemoration of his birth in ten years.

Moreover, the real meaning of the "balance" was soon revealed. In 1970, the Brezhnev leadership placed a flattering marble bust of Stalin on his gravesite immediately behind the Lenin Mausoleum, where his body had once been on view. Readily accessible, it was regularly adorned with flowers. The bust may not have signified his unconditional rehabilitation or a restoration of the Stalin cult, but it exonerated him of the criminal indictment brought by Khrushchev. Governments do not erect monuments, even small ones, to people they consider to be criminals.

Three episodes involving names familiar to readers symbolized how fully Khrushchev's successors repudiated his anti-Stalinist legacy. In 1964, the most celebrated Gulag writer, Solzhenitsyn, was a nominee for a Lenin Prize. In 1974, he was arrested and deported from the Soviet Union. In 1962, a Khrushchev aide indicated that Bukharin, Stalin's most important political victim, might be exonerated, telling a conference of historians, "Neither Bukharin nor [his ally] Rykov was, of course, a spy or a terrorist." In 1977, a Central Committee official informed Bukharin's family that "the criminal charges on . . . which he was convicted have not been removed."[7] The announcement in effect rehabilitated the notorious Moscow Trials of the 1930s and thus the Stalinist terror.

The fate of Molotov, the senior living Stalinist most harshly indicted by Khrushchev, was equally indicative. In 1962, Molotov was expelled from the Communist Party, creating the impression that he would be put on trial for crimes of the Stalin era. He then disappeared from public view. In 1984, the Politburo readmitted Molotov to the Party. It was not a casual decision. Brezhnev's heir, Konstantin Chernenko, the last Soviet leader before Gorbachev, personally received the ninety-three-year-old, still unrepentant Stalinist in his office to congratulate him.[8] Both men, it was said, were teary-eyed.

Those episodes were publicly known, but only later did archive documents reveal how much Khrushchev's successors continued to hate and revile him in private. "Not one enemy," they agreed, "brought us so much grief as did Khrushchev." Suslov added, "We still have not eliminated everything that resulted from Khrushchev." They were particularly offended by the "shameful outrages Khrushchev permitted in relation to Stalin" and by his support for the tyrant's victims, whom they referred to as "scum" and "social riff-raff." Khrushchev, they implied, had exonerated them "illegally." Brezhnev complained, for example, that Solzhenitsyn, whom he maintained had been justly imprisoned under Stalin, had been "rehabilitated by two people—Shatunovskaya and Snegov."(Brezhnev was not alone: the new head of the KGB,

Vladimir Semichastny, agreed that Solzhenitsyn had been rightfully convicted.)[9]

In that spirit, the Brezhnev years were much better times for many agents of Stalin's terror. Those who died before Khrushchev's revelations, like Vyshinsky and Ulrikh, remained in their honored burial sites. Those imprisoned under Khrushchev were often released early, including one "hangman" responsible for more than a thousand executions. Many of them apparently had their ranks, awards, and pensions restored.[10]

Innumerable NKVD men and other victimizers who had escaped punishment went on to esteemed careers, some as academics and as censors, and later were buried in honor, like Yudin and Mitin, who remained the editor of the most prestigious philosophical journal until 1968. When Kliment Voroshilov, Stalin's chief accomplice in the massacre of thousands of military officers, died in 1969, he was given a state funeral and a place in the Kremlin Wall. Suslov, who died in 1982, was awarded an even grander farewell, the most elaborate official funeral since Stalin's and a nearby gravesite in the grassy pantheon behind the Mausoleum.

The sanitized biography of Vyshinsky's right-hand man, Lev Sheinin, particularly interested me. Working in the NKVD archive in the 1990s, I came across detailed evidence of Sheinin's personal role, inside Lubyanka Prison, in preparing tormented victims, including Bukharin, for the falsified trials of the 1930s. Sheinin's loyalties—he also attended executions as Vyshinsky's surrogate—were clear from his praise for one of the most brutal NKVD torturers as a "dear friend and wonderful person." By the late 1960s, Sheinin had reemerged as an acclaimed author of detective stories—the genre also favored, readers will recall, by another retired victimizer, Andrei Sverdlov—and of a memoir relating his career as a justice-seeking "investigator" for the Procuracy.[11] Sheinin's official obituaries, like the others, were uniformly admiring and silent about his role in the terror.

Accordingly, the years from Khrushchev's downfall to the rise of Gorbachev were not good ones for most of Stalin's victims. During those two decades, unlike the former zek who wrote to Khrushchev, "Thanks to you, I do not leave life a slandered woman,"[12] many Gulag returnees died without having been formally exonerated of the criminal charges on which they had been convicted. As a result, the "stain" often adhered to their children and grandchildren, passing on obstacles to their own futures in the Soviet system. The same was true for close relatives of the millions who had perished in the terror and not been posthumously rehabilitated. In this respect, the number of collateral victims continued to grow.

Not even all of the returnees who had been officially exonerated under Khrushchev felt secure after his ouster. Many soon sensed, as some were told by officials, "The rehabilitated are no longer in fashion," and, more ominously, "Far too many were rehabilitated."[13] Considering the staged trial of two anti-Stalinist writers, Andrei Sinyavsky and Yuli Daniel, in 1966, the refurbishing of Stalin's official reputation, and the reappearance of "enemies of the people" in sanctioned historical literature, former zeks hardly needed to be informed that their status had changed. For several of my returnee friends, the bust placed on Stalin's grave was enough to induce a feeling of "psychological execution."

Until Khrushchev's overthrow, the presence of Shatunovskaya, Snegov, and other freed zeks in his entourage had restrained anti-returnee attitudes among lower-ranking Soviet officials. After 1964, they no longer felt so constrained. (Mikoyan, the other patron of returnees, "retired" not long after Khrushchev.) Snegov, whom a Party functionary once asked to intervene with Khrushchev on his behalf, became a special target of vindictive reprisals. The instigator seems to have been Mikhail Suslov, a powerful member of the new leadership, whose complicity in the terror Snegov had uncovered.

Other officials threatened nonconformist children of victims, as one had warned Igor Pyatnitsky, with the "fate" of their parents. More generally, as the Brezhnev years grew into a long winter of conservative reaction, more and more returnees rehabilitated under Khrushchev "no longer felt rehabilitated."[14]

Little may have changed for the majority of surviving victims who had lived in obscure, conformist ways since being freed from the Gulag. But those whose hopes and activities had been aroused by Khrushchev's policies now had to reconsider their prospects. Among the returnees I met during the first six years I collected material for this book in Moscow, from 1976 to 1982, more than half had lost all hope of living to see Stalin's terror fully exposed, their stories made known, and justice carried out in the Soviet Union. They no longer had any faith in the system, now viewing Khrushchev as "a miracle that won't happen again."

By the early 1980s, when emigration had become possible for Soviet citizens claiming Jewish ancestry, many of Stalin's surviving victims had left the country. Their ties to the Soviet Union had long since been dissipated. But others departed whose existence outside Russia seemed unimaginable, at least to me. Yuri Gastyev, whose post-Gulag life was rooted in Moscow's nonconformist circles, emigrated to the United States in 1981, where he died in 1993. So did his friend Naum Korzhavin, also a former zek and an admired poet with deep Russian roots; despite visits to post-Soviet Russia, he still lives in Boston. Even Tanya Bayeva, whose Moscow apartment had been a haven for Stalin's victims and for recent dissidents, eventually moved to the United States with her husband and young son. Her friends bid her farewell with their customary toast, "Let us drink to our hopeless cause."

Other victims of Stalin's terror, however, continued to believe in the Soviet system's redemptive possibilities, though for different reasons. Political intellectuals who had once been Communist Party members, such as Roy Medvedev, Yevgeny Gnedin, Mikhail

Baitalsky, and Lev Kopelev, remained convinced—or at least continued to hope—that a new generation of anti-Stalinist reformers might one day emerge in its leadership.[15] Forbidden in public discourse, that possibility was a constant subject of Roy's writings published abroad, our frequent conversations, larger gatherings at Gnedin's apartment, and indeed of serious discussions in kitchens across Moscow and other Soviet cities during the Brezhnev years.

For family members of executed Soviet founders like Anna Larina, Natalya Rykova, Yuri Tomsky, Kamil Ikramov, and Anton Antonov-Ovseyenko, on the other hand, belief that the system would some day right Stalinist wrongs was primarily an expression of loyalty to their loved ones who had created it. Larina's devotion became legendary. In 1937, on the eve of Bukharin's arrest, she had memorized his last "Testament," with its certainty that "a future generation of Party leaders" would "vindicate me."[16] During her twenty years in the Gulag, Anna silently repeated the text, like a prayer; and in 1961, hoping her husband would be exonerated, recited it to a sympathetic Shatunovskaya at Party headquarters. It was finally published in 1987, to official acclaim, under Gorbachev.

Stalin's victims who still hoped for full redemption clung to the idea that Khrushchev had not been an aberration—and to the memory of his years in power. When he died in September 1971, after seven years of imposed near-isolation with his family at a dacha outside Moscow, a crowd of former zeks and children of victims tried to defy the Kremlin's efforts to prevent access to his funeral at Novodevichy Cemetery. (Of his former political colleagues, only Mikoyan sent a wreath.) Later, so many flowers were anonymously placed on Khrushchev's grave, marked by a large white and black monument commissioned by his family to reflect his dual role in history, the government closed Novodevichy to the public.

Less known is that a number of Stalin's victims managed to visit Khrushchev during his last years, including Mikhail

Shatrov, Pyotr Yakir, and Tanya Bayeva. Himself now an official non-person and a kind of victim, the man who had once ruled a superpower warmly welcomed them. In mild weather, they sat around the dacha's picnic table, the rotund Khrushchev at the head in a peasant blouse and straw brimmed-hat. They discussed many things, but especially Khrushchev's pride in what he had achieved while in power and his profound regrets for what he had done under Stalin and not done after the dictator's death. Khrushchev remained steadfastly loyal to Solzhenitsyn, for example, remarking affectionately, "I'm crazy and he's crazy," reading contraband copies of the author's banned novels, and observing with pride, "They don't give Nobel Prizes for nothing."[17] Khrushchev too hoped that his "real" successor, another anti-Stalinist, would eventually come to power.

What the fallen leader told his visitors in that connection was echoed in two publications which appeared years later. One was the transcript of a tense 1970 meeting Khrushchev was summoned to attend with representatives of the Brezhnev leadership. They threatened to punish him for sending his uncensored memoirs, dictated privately, to the West. (His son chose another Gulag survivor, a shadowy entrepreneur named Viktor Louis, who had been released and rehabilitated in 1956, to smuggle the tapes to the United States.) Gravely ill but defiant, Khrushchev responded by denouncing the current leaders for repudiating the anti-Stalinism he had enacted at two Party congresses, reminding them "how many people perished, how many were shot" under Stalin, and by returning to the theme that contributed to his overthrow: "Murderers must be exposed."[18]

In those memoirs, which are now available in full, Khrushchev addressed the possibility of an eventual successor who would embrace his anti-Stalinist legacy. In the 1970s, most Western specialists thought it could not happen, but Khrushchev took a long and optimistic view, as he did with his visitors:

I regret, of course, that ... during the years I was in the
leadership of the country, I did not complete this. But it's okay.
What one person does not do, another will do later. And if
not the next person, then another, because a just cause will
never die.[19]

During the repressive Brezhnev years, Stalin's victims who
shared Khrushchev's optimism nonetheless had to decide whether
or not to risk fighting for that goal. Taking into account what
they had already suffered and the possible consequences for their
families, especially their children, people naturally made different
choices. One established writer was so frightened by the KGB's
search of a friend's apartment, he burned his own play about terror-
era victims and victimizers. (He rewrote it in 1988.) Learning that
the head of the KGB had called her memoirs "a libelous work
that helps our enemies," Eugenia Ginzburg also burned her
manuscript, but soon recomposed it and let it be published in the
West a decade before she died in 1977.[20]

Snegov, after a brief period of adamantly protesting Stalin's
rehabilitation—at one meeting he defended a historian under
attack for criticizing the despot's wartime conduct as Khrushchev
had done—retreated into passive seclusion. Encouraged by
their families, others, as I noted in the preceding chapter,
devoted themselves secretly to their memoirs. Some, like Larina,
Shatunovskaya, Ikramov, and Bukharin's younger brother,
Vladimir, wrote or dictated only "for the drawer" in faint hope of
a future Thaw. Still others, like Gnedin, Baitalsky, and Yakir, wrote
for eventual circulation in typescript and, when the chance arose,
for publication abroad.

More than a few victims were too determined for any degree
of silence. Renewed state censorship of the Stalin era turned Roy
and Zhores Medvedev into political outcasts from their original
professions at home but into widely acclaimed historians in the

West. Antonov-Ovseyenko, as he often reminded me, was on a mission to "unmask Stalin's hangmen and their heirs in the KGB." (When secret policemen searched his apartment in 1982, he shouted at them repeatedly, "I'll expose you too in my book!") Solzhenitsyn and Kopelev waged their wars of words against the past and the present so unrelentingly they were banished from the Soviet Union. Vasily Aksyonov, Ginzburg's son, finally left for much the same reason.

There was, however, a course between defiance and silence. With the terror ended and the Party-state's controls less encompassing, Soviet writers could sometimes publish indirect or elliptical commentaries on Stalin-era subjects in cracks in the system of censorship or, as was said, "between the lines." In the 1970s, Leonid Petrovsky and Antonov-Ovseyenko managed to publish biographies of their executed fathers. Both books were heavily censored, with no indication of how their subjects had actually died. In addition, Leonid's was so abridged it emerged as barely more than a pamphlet, and in faraway Soviet Kazakhstan, while Anton had to publish his under a pseudonym.[21] Both agonized over their compromises but were consoled by having reintroduced their fathers to the public.

Similarly, a remarkable number of sanctioned poets of the Soviet 1970s were freed zeks who embedded allusions to their Gulag experiences in their lines, as Yuri Aikhenvald was doing in the plays he translated. Those writers—among them, Nikolai Zabolotsky, Anatoly Zhigulin, Boris Ruchev, Andrei Aldan-Semyonov, and Yaroslav Smelyakov—are unknown to most Western readers but were popular among educated Russians. Other returnees who knew those poets had also "sat" under Stalin pored over their publications for oblique references to their own camp experiences. (My lame effort to formulate their pursuit as a Gulag board game fell flat.)

The most notable between-the-lines writers on the terror, though, were two famous sons of prominent Stalin victims: the playwright Shatrov and the novelist Yuri Trifonov. Most of Shatrov's plays were set in the pre-Stalinist period of Soviet history. They featured dramatic events, but necessarily without their leading, still un-rehabilitated protagonists such as Bukharin, Rykov, Tomsky, and Trotsky. I sometimes wondered if the censors understood that Shatrov's audiences could not only read fluently between the lines but fill in his omissions without prompting.

In *The Bolsheviks*, for example, which Anna Larina took me to see at a packed Moscow theater in the late 1970s, Shatrov focused on an impassioned debate among Lenin's comrades following an attempt on his life in 1918, which left him seriously wounded: did it justify unleashing terror against the Party's opponents? A remarkably candid, if somewhat abstract, discussion unfolded on that Brezhnev-era stage about the morality, efficacy, and consequences of political terror.[22] More interesting to me was the parallel drama in the audience, whose gasps of approval and indignation expressed the enduring trauma of Stalin's terror just below the surface of Soviet society.

Trifonov's impact was considerably greater. A masterful writer whose novels reached wider audiences than did Shatrov's plays, his subject was the Stalinist terror itself, the act of betrayal, and its consequences for lives in the 1970s. In two novels published during the Brezhnev era, Trifonov explored the conscience-stricken memories awakened in successful Soviet citizens who had made fateful choices involving friends and colleagues during the terror. As Lev Kopelev, a survivor and a literary man, observed, Trifonov "gets everything in. He only doesn't mention things that are specifically forbidden. He assumes the reader already knows what he is alluding to."[23]

Some Soviet intellectuals criticized Trifonov for remaining within the constraints of censorship, but Gulag returnees admired what he published. They also knew his personal drama. Born in 1925, Trifonov, like many of his characters, was an orphan of the terror, a generation whose members sometimes made choices they later regretted. In 1951, Trifonov won a Stalin prize for his conformist first novel. In the twilight of Khrushchev's Thaw, he repented for that "betrayal" of his parents by publishing a remarkably candid book about his father's fate.[24] His novels of the 1970s were even more broadly and profoundly redemptive. In this respect, Trifonov, who died in 1981, was a forerunner of the historical, political, and personal repentance that would be a major feature of the Gorbachev years.

Finally, there was the important role played by Stalin's victims and their family members in the Soviet dissident movement and in the uncensored manuscripts known as *samizdat*. Typescripts passed from hand to hand grew into a large phenomenon in the mid- and late 1960s in the form of petitions protesting the Kremlin's rehabilitation of Stalin. Many of the people readers have already encountered in this book were among the initial contributors—Gnedin, Kopelev, Ikramov, the Medvedev brothers, Antonov-Ovseyenko, Aikhenvald, Igor Pyatnitsky, Yuli Kim, Gastyev, Yakir, Petrovsky, Yuri Larin, Tanya Bayeva, and Mikhail Baitalsky.

Still more, as the terror and its victims vanished from the Soviet official media, those subjects became central features of *samizdat*, supplemented by the growing volume of manuscripts published abroad and smuggled back into the country. Readers of uncensored writings may have numbered only in the thousands, but they were enough to pass on knowledge of the Stalin years, especially to a younger generation that came to age during Brezhnev's long reign. Here too the most important books were ones by terror-era victims—Roy Medvedev's *Let History Judge*, Solzhenitsyn's *The Gulag Archipelago* and his related novels, and the memoir-accounts by Ginzburg, Kopelev, and other survivors.

Indeed, by the early 1970s, when sporadic protest writings had given rise to a larger dissident movement demanding fundamental changes in the Soviet system, its three most prominent representatives were men strongly affected by the Stalinist terror.[25] On the ideological left, speaking for a social-democratic Marxism-Leninism, was Roy Medvedev, whose father had died in the Gulag. On the right, representing Russian nationalist traditions, was the former zek Solzhenitsyn. And between them was the nuclear scientist Andrei Sakharov, whose mother-in-law had been freed under Khrushchev.

Most of the victims-turned-dissidents I knew endured their past and subsequent lives, but one did not. The tragedy of Pyotr Yakir, the son of a top army commander shot in 1937, played out in the long shadow of Stalin's terror. After seventeen years in the Gulag, from age fourteen, Yakir was freed by Khrushchev. Burly, outgoing, and passionately devoted to historical justice, he was an exceptionally bold returnee but also a man tormented by memories of the Gulag and increasingly by alcoholism. The overthrow of Khrushchev, who had personally befriended him, transformed Yakir into a leading organizer of the dissident movement's clandestine and public activities, as well as coauthor, with his friend Leonid Petrovsky, of passionate anti-Stalinist manifestoes.

As a result, in June 1972, Yakir was arrested. The head of the KGB, and future Soviet leader, Yuri Andropov, personally supervised the case. (It is said that Andropov waited until Pyotr's mother, a Gulag survivor and widow of the rehabilitated commander, died a few months before.) Exactly what the KGB said and did to Yakir in a Moscow prison remains unknown— they may have threatened to reveal his forced collaboration with the NKVD in the 1940s—but fourteen months later he emerged on national television repudiating his dissident role and having given information that led to more than a hundred searches and interrogations as well as other arrests. Yakir's own punishment was relatively light, reduced to three years of exile in a city not far from Moscow. He was then permitted to return to the capital. A chronically ill recluse, he died, at fifty-nine, in 1982, on the same day Brezhnev was buried.

Many of Yakir's fellow dissidents harshly condemned him for having been "broken," but very few victims of Stalin's terror did so. Anna Larina, who knew Yakir and his mother in the Gulag, always remembered him as "the marvelous doomed boy Petya Yakir."[26] She never spoke of him except with admiration and affection. The usually forthcoming Tanya Bayeva, a close friend of Yakir's daughter, Irina, and her husband, Yuli Kim, refused to tell me what she knew about his personal tragedy and also never spoke critically of him. Another Gulag returnee would say only, "They could find ways to do it to any of us."

Looking back, no one questions the significance of the dissident movement, though there is little agreement about its larger role. Some Russians insist it brought about the democratic changes that began in the Soviet Union under Gorbachev in the late 1980s. Others argue that the essential factor was the new leader and his supporters in the ruling elite. Having known dissidents and members of Gorbachev's inner circle, but also as a historian, I hold the latter view. In Russia, political reform has always begun at the top, with those who have the power to initiate it.

But dissidents did make an important contribution. By keeping alive the memory of the terror and the anti-Stalinism of the Khrushchev years, and by advocating democratic and other heretical ideas so boldly and persistently, they helped to prepare the Soviet political establishment for the changes that followed the conservative Brezhnev era. Gorbachev acknowledged as much by enabling one-time dissidents to participate in sanctioned politics and by removing the ban on their writings.

In that respect, Stalin's victims, out of official favor and banished from public view for twenty years, contributed to their own reappearance, a kind of second great return, this time much more fully and warmly supported by the Soviet government. Given their age and years of abuse, the majority of Gulag returnees probably did not live to witness that historic development.

The Gorbachev years are remembered primarily for having led to the end of the Soviet Union, but they also brought Stalin's victims, for the first and perhaps last time, to the forefront of political life. In the late 1980s, "the entire country," according to a sociologist, was "reflecting on the Stalin phenomenon."[27] Graphic public accounts of the mass terror far exceeded the sporadic, fragmentary revelations under Khrushchev, as did the scope of historical justice and the number of individual exonerations. An elderly Gulag survivor—freed but not rehabilitated in the 1950s— later called Gorbachev "St. Mikhail, our redeemer."

But the overriding mission of the new leader was much larger. The Soviet reformation attempted by Gorbachev from 1985 to the end of 1991, or Perestroika, sought to replace the existing monopolistic controls imposed by Stalin with a substantially democratized and marketized system. In order to overcome enormous opposition, Gorbachev had to de-legitimize Stalin-era dogmas and taboos that sanctified the current order. For that, he had to expose, much more fully than Khrushchev had, the crimes committed from 1929 to 1953. He therefore needed an alternative Soviet history. There was only one, the market-oriented, less-draconian NEP 1920s, whose full recovery was still blocked by Stalin's criminalization of that decade's representative political figure, Nikolai Bukharin.

Reclaiming Bukharin was one of the first struggles Gorbachev faced behind the scenes after taking office in 1985. (Even the future maximalist Boris Yeltsin, then a junior Party leader, objected that it was "too early," but Gorbachev insisted, "It is already late.") Only in 1987 was Gorbachev able to publicly embrace, and radicalize, Khrushchev's long-banned anti-Stalinism and hold Stalin personally responsible for "real crimes." He did so unconditionally: "We cannot and should not ever forgive or justify what happened." In November, in a televised speech to the nation, Gorbachev personally rehabilitated the names of both Bukharin and Khrushchev.[28]

As a result, a "Bukharinist Boom," in the words of two Russian historians, exploded in Soviet politics and culture.[29] From an arch-enemy of the nation, Bukharin was transformed into one of its greatest heroes—even into Lenin's real successor. The "Boom" included hundreds of mass-media eulogies, new editions of his writings and speeches, admiring studies of his ideas, three full-length biographies, in addition to Anna Larina's best-selling memoirs, a year-long exhibit at the Museum of the Revolution, three feature films, and an array of novels, plays, poems, and visual artifacts, from lapel buttons to paintings.

The effect was to cast Bukharin as Stalin's Victim Number One but also, Gorbachev's top aide recalled, to "open the sluice gates" of historical truth-telling. As the gradual end of censorship, or glasnost, spread through the Soviet media with tales of the long terror, often told by survivors themselves, countless names of other prominent victims also returned in newspapers, radio and television broadcasts, and special collections of articles.[30] With the Soviet publication of *The Gulag Archipelago*, 1990 was sometimes called "The Year of Solzhenitsyn," though I thought of it, and the preceding twenty-four months, as the time Stalin's victims truly returned. (Solzhenitsyn himself returned to Russia only in 1994.)

Nor were unknown victims overlooked. Khrushchev's commissions had taken eight years to rehabilitate about 700,000 individuals. In two years, Gorbachev's exonerated more than a million, and in 1991 he issued a blanket presidential decree rehabilitating all of Stalin's remaining victims. Meanwhile, justice was also being pursued below. In 1988, a grassroots movement, widely reported in the press, began uncovering mass graves of people shot in the late 1930s and early 1940s; by 1991, nearly a hundred had been discovered. (The site at Donskoi Cemetery, where Sasha Milchakov showed me the crematorium, was designated "Common Grave No.1." The tombstone reads: "Here Are Buried the Remains of Innocent Tormented and Executed Victims of Political Repressions. May They Never Be Forgotten.")

For the first time, Stalin's victims acquired independent organizations to represent them. The most important was created by people of several generations. In 1987, young anti-Stalinist activists revived Khrushchev's 1961 call for a national monument to victims of the terror. In 1988, well-known, middle-aged intellectuals and other public figures, backed by petitions with tens of thousands of signatures and by Gorbachev's endorsement, established the Memorial Society, which soon had affiliates around the country.[31] Its purpose was to identify and commemorate the dead but also to help the dwindling number of survivors, partly through public donations. When charitable bank accounts were announced, the response, mostly in small bills, was nation-wide.

Too many victims I knew in the 1970s died before the rise of Gorbachev, but others were alive and ready to play their new roles. I was happiest, of course, for Anna Larina. Published in Moscow in 1988, her memoirs of her life with Bukharin, and then in the Gulag, made her the country's most famous political widow. "Imagine," she remarked with bemused astonishment, "this old zek is a media star at seventy-four!" Her son, Yuri, political obstacles removed, finally emerged as an acclaimed artist. Bukharin's daughter, Svetlana Gurvich, though still nervously, soon followed as a historian.

Others I knew came to the fore in their own ways. Shatrov's plays, *Dictatorship of Conscience* and *Onward, Onward, Onward!*, made the theater, as was said, a "virtual parliament" before

Gorbachev inaugurated a real one in 1989. Roy Medvedev and Andrei Sakharov were elected to the new legislature. Leonid Petrovsky, while writing the unabridged truth about his anti-Stalinist father, seemed to be on every Perestroika barricade. Milchakov's articles spearheaded the hunt for mass graves, and he and Yuri Aikhenvald, no longer anonymous, were among Memorial's founders. Antonov-Ovseyenko's prosecutorial articles about Stalin and "Beria's gang" filled the press. Lev Razgon's Gulag stories established him as a leading writer and television personality. And a mortally ill Kamil Ikramov finished his book about his family tragedy before he died in 1989.[32]

Stalin's victims, "at once tragic and sacred," now had the sympathetic attention of the nation, or at least of those Soviet officials and citizens who supported Gorbachev's reforms. The second return of the survivors, and the dead, was a ubiquitous feature of Perestroika, from movie and television screens, large museum exhibits, and "Evenings of Remembrance" to outdoor meetings. Here is an abridged account of two characteristic events in Moscow, in March 1989, written for *The Nation* by my wife, Katrina vanden Heuvel:

> Anti-Stalinism was the main theme of the epidemic of Moscow *mitingi*. "A Political Spectacle" was staged at the Institute of International Relations. Produced by student impressarios and Memorial, the evening featured speeches, films, and fledgling rock-and-roll bands. It attracted more than a thousand people. Speakers included Anna Larina, the son-in-law of Khrushchev, whose reputation is soaring, and a writer who described the newly discovered NKVD killing fields.
>
> Between the speakers and clips from the anti-Stalinist film *Repentance*, the bands played songs, with such titles as "Gulag Archipelago" and "NKVD." During the intermission, the audience flowed into the institute's foyer, where Memorial

had organized an exhibit of photographs and materials documenting the Stalinist terror, and of prospective designs for the monument honoring the victims.

The next day, Memorial staged a rally in Gorky Park that drew a crowd of about three thousand. An array of people streamed into the park, aged survivors of Stalin's camps alongside young couples pushing baby strollers.[33]

For the first time, special attention also focused on the children of the terror, many orphaned by executions and Gulag deaths, who continued to be collateral victims. Some still knew nothing about what had happened to their parents, and others who had partial knowledge remained tormented by what they did not know. Newspapers soon filled with letters appealing for information, like this one from a man in the city of Novosibirsk: "In 1937, I lost my father and grandfather. In 1956, I learned of their death and posthumous rehabilitation. But my conscience has known no peace all these years. What kind of son and grandson am I if I cannot honor their graves?"[34]

Prompted by Gorbachev's policies, high-ranking officials promised to help. Delegations of victims were received by the speaker of the new legislature, Anatoly Lukyanov, and separately by an unusually sympathetic KGB general, Anatoly Krayushkin. (The intellectual Krayushkin, who originally wanted to be an actor, and looked the part, certainly helped me when I knew him later in his capacity of head of the secret police archives, until he was fired in 1995.)[35] For relatives of the vanished, however, little specific information resulted from those meetings. Memorial made such discoveries a major part of its program, but more information came initially from the efforts of two remarkable, and unexpected, individuals than from any institution.

One was himself the son of a victim. Sasha Milchakov's own father, readers will recall, returned from the Gulag in the 1950s, but the son never stopped thinking about those who did not come back, or about their families. Thirty years later, Gorbachev's initiatives unleashed Milchakov, a small, disheveled, incongruously jovial man in his mid-fifties, who wore an ill-matching suit and tie even while trudging through muddy gravesites, perhaps to assure alarmed secret police and cemetery authorities that he was a professional journalist. Following him around, I thought of Sasha as the most determined seeker of the terror's lost, forgotten, and unknown dead.

Beginning in 1988, Milchakov created a sensation with pioneering articles exposing the NKVD's mass graves in Moscow. Boundlessly energetic, he turned then to the fates of individual victims, prying out of the NKVD's successor, the KGB, exact dates of executions, burial places, and even prison mug shots. Opposed by most KGB officials but assisted by a few, Milchakov's success was astonishing. When his "Lists of the Shot," initially with dozens of names and then hundreds, began appearing in a popular Moscow newspaper, relatives of people who had vanished fifty years before eagerly awaited each installment in the hope of finally learning what happened to them. Most waited in vain, but many did not.[36]

Their other hero, a jeans-clad young man in his early twenties, barely more than a student, was even more unexpected. In 1986, Dmitri Yurasov, a junior archivist at the Soviet Supreme Court, came across records of millions of unknown cases dating back to the 1930s. The files contained detailed information about victims and death sentences, as well as desperate pleas written by doomed prisoners. (One was the director Meyerhold's graphic account of his torture quoted earlier in this book.) For a year, Yurasov secretly compiled index cards on some 123,000 cases, which he smuggled home until he was found out and fired.

After making public his sensational discoveries, the tall "archive kid," with edgy good-looks and a somber manner, became a glasnost celebrity. By 1989, Yurasov was a frequent guest of many people I knew—Medvedev, Shatrov, Petrovsky, Ikramov, Antonov-Ovseyenko, Anna Larina, at whose apartment I first met him, and more. (In 1990, I initiated his speaking tour of American universities, including my own, Princeton.) But Yurasov's relationship with the many people who queried him about long-missing relatives was special. He tried to reply to each of them. Though later embroiled in ugly disputes with former supporters, for these people he was always "our Dima."

The intense spotlight on Stalin's victims inexorably revived the search, officially halted in the early 1960s, for their victimizers, as well as calls for new trials. "Those who murdered people are still alive!" declared the editor of the most popular Soviet magazine of the late 1980s, "There must be a second Nuremberg!" In that spirit, journalists went looking for surviving "hangmen on pension" who had participated in the terror fifty years before. The result was a handful of aged men, a few still insisting their victims had been "enemies of the people," or they had been "obeying orders," others cowering fearfully in their apartments barely able to understand the charges against them or remember their crimes. (Years later, one former junior "hangman" finally expressed public remorse.)[37]

Few victims I knew took much satisfaction from the spectacle, and none favored actual trials. Some supported the idea of a posthumous, or symbolic, trial of Stalin, and all were advocates of the ongoing media trial of the Stalin era, with its far-reaching discussion of national "conscience and repentance." Most agreed with Roy Medvedev, though, that meaningful judgment could be passed "only by the court of history."[38] Meanwhile, influenced by their experiences as collateral victims, Anna Larina and others worried about the innocent families of the low-level accomplices now being pursued. "What kind of life can they have," she asked, "if the names, photographs, and addresses of their fathers and grandfathers are exposed in the press?"

Larina and I became involved in two such cases. When my biography of Bukharin was published in Moscow in 1989, the only young Bukharinist who survived Stalin's massacre, Valentin Astrov, now ninety-one, suddenly emerged to respond to the book's suggestion (since confirmed) that he saved himself by giving false testimony against his friends. Evidently prompted by his family "to establish the truth," Astrov published a long letter in a leading newspaper justifying his conduct.[39] The editor urged Larina and me to reply, shaming Astrov even more. Neither of us had the heart for it. (Afterwards, when Yuri Aikhenvald telephoned Astrov to curse him for betraying Yuri's parents, he had the impression the old man did not remember what he had done.)

Our experience with the sixty-five-year-old daughter of Bukharin's interrogator in Lubyanka Prison, Lazar Kogan, was more wrenching. Despite his direct participation in her husband's destruction, Anna felt some sympathy for Kogan and his family. As Larina later recalled, when she met with the young NKVD captain briefly at Lubyanka following Bukharin's arrest in 1937, he suddenly "firmly pressed my hand. I glanced at his face and was surprised to see unspeakable remorse in his eyes."[40] It was part of the reason Larina told the daughter, when I brought them together many years later, that Bukharin and Kogan were "both victims."

My own conflicted feelings grew the more I learned from Kogan's daughter, whose life in a Stalin-era orphanage and later in a desultory small town had been bleak. Ten-years-old in 1938, when her father disappeared from his hospital sick-bed—he was shot in 1939, almost exactly a year after Bukharin—she clung to her childhood memories and love for him. With faint hope that a "NKVD hangman" would ever be given any measure of rehabilitation, all that remained for her were faded photographs of Kogan with his wife and young daughter—and among fellow officers—and a short hand-written letter from him.

Kogan wrote the letter on her birthday in August 1937, while under intense pressure to prepare the still uncooperative Bukharin for his forthcoming trial and shortly after being awarded an Order of Lenin for his "services." When the daughter showed me the letter, I read it in silence, without any outward reaction. Readers may judge it, and what it reveals about those times, for themselves:

> My Dear, Beloved Daughter!
> I congratulate you on your birthday. I warmly embrace and kiss you. Live and grow together with our sunny country, the only, most beautiful, soviet country. In our country, everything is for you. And your Papa lives and works for YOU. And the Order of Lenin is for YOU and for ALL THE CHILDREN. Grow and be a worthy daughter of your country and of its leader, Comrade STALIN.
>
> Papa

Scholarly objectivity is important, but mine was tested during the Gorbachev years. Katrina and I, our entry visas renewed, were again living in the Soviet Union for several months a year. As one of the few Western scholars who had foreseen the possibility of a new anti-Stalinist leadership, I wanted to apply the same kind of detached analysis to Gorbachev's unfolding reforms. But in Moscow, with the political rediscovery of Bukharin, the Soviet publication of my book had become a heralded symbol of those dramatic changes. I was overwhelmed by requests to give interviews to the media and to speak at public events.

I tried to draw a line between my analysis of the fast-moving developments and my long involvement with people whose lives were being transformed by them. But where was the line? (A question I occasionally discussed with Len Karpinsky, who having been readmitted to the Party—he quit in 1991—was now a highly respected writer and editor.) In 1989, I suddenly received an official invitation to speak briefly on Soviet national television from Red Square during the annual May Day parade. My initial instinct was to decline; the proposal seemed preposterous. But Anna Larina and several other Gulag survivors from my past had a different opinion, which they pressed on me in a characteristic way: "Steve, you say you are merely an accidental person in everything that is happening today, but you are wrong. It is our common fate."

And so, with Katrina and my son, Andrew, at my side, I was escorted to a festooned Red Square crammed with thousands of spectators, to a spot alongside the Lenin Mausoleum. Other speakers were already gathered, including an improbably young activist who had just defeated the local Party boss for mayor of Volgograd, once Stalingrad. Gorbachev and his associates stood above us, atop the Mausoleum, reviewing the three-hour parade. When my turn came to speak to tens of millions of television viewers, I tried to be professorial (and grammatical in Russian), expounding vaguely on historical alternatives. But a few days after, I knew I had blurred the line when a Russian parliamentary candidate asked me to speak for him at a rally. I firmly declined and retreated to the political sidelines.

I felt no need, however, to constrain my sympathies for those Stalinist victims whose sufferings were finally being publicly acknowledged. With unambiguous satisfaction, I participated in events in their honor, sometimes with Anna Larina at Evenings of Remembrance. Many Gulag survivors I had known years earlier, when their existence had been bare and unrecognized, seemed exalted by their new status. Larina's son saw that kind of renewal in his mother. As Yuri later recalled, in a PBS television film I made (with Rosemarie Reed) about Larina, *Widow of the Revolution*, "I was so proud of her. She had been humiliated for so long. And now she was so dignified."

There were also more private moments of emotion. On a memorable evening in 1988, Katrina, Larina, and I attended a Moscow stage adaptation of Ginzburg's Gulag memoirs. As scenes of her arrest and interrogation, and fearful concerns for her family, played out on the stage, elderly survivors in the theater reacted spontaneously, not with murmurs, as at Shatrov's allusive play a decade before, but with clearly audible interjections: "Yes, exactly, that's how it was!" "That's what they did to me!" "The bastards!" Anna sat silently, nodding her head slightly, her eyes dry. Mine were not.

But another public event, in 1989, the first to honor Khrushchev since his official disgrace in 1964, epitomized the extraordinary blending of history, politics, and personal memories during the Gorbachev years. It was held in a large prestigious auditorium in the center of Moscow. Sitting on the speakers dais with Larina, Medvedev, and several other people I had interviewed in secret only a few years earlier, I saw many former zeks in the brightly lit, overflowing hall. No less amazed than I was by the historic changes we were witnessing, they were finally able to pay homage to the man who had freed them. Some were weeping.

At a reception afterwards, journalists began arguing over Khrushchev's contradictory role. By then, most people knew the dark side of his career—the blood on his own hands, his failure to tell the whole truth, his ban on Pasternak's *Dr. Zhivago* and Vasily Grossman's masterwork, *Life and Fate*, his own repressive measures after 1956, which refilled several labor camps, and more. But the gratitude of Gulag returnees present was undiminished. Virtually in one voice, they echoed what Yevgeny Gnedin had said to me in the 1970s: "I know all the bad things Khrushchev did. But he gave me back my life and my family, and he gave me a pension. What more could I ask of him?" The poet Anna Akhmatova had put it more succinctly: "I am a Khrushchevist."[41]

A great many members of the Soviet elite and ordinary citizens did not, however, admire Khrushchev—or the man who reclaimed him. By 1990, opposition to Gorbachev's Perestroika had spread across the country, as its political and economic reforms turned a once-sacred history into a "martyrology," threatened the job security and living standards of millions of people, and deprived hundreds of thousands of Party and state officials of their authority, while also provoking demands for more radical changes. For most of these people and the forces representing them, Gorbachev's policies were acts of betrayal and his anti-Stalinism an "ideology of former zeks."[42]

The latter allegation had no political basis, but it did contain a sliver of historical truth. A remarkable number of Gorbachev's high-level associates were relatives of Stalin's victims, among them his foreign minister, Eduard Shevardnadze; the powerful Party boss who helped bring Gorbachev to power, Yegor Ligachev; and Boris Yeltsin. Still more, Gorbachev's own peasant grandfathers had been arrested in the 1930s. They were eventually released, but not his wife's grandfather, who died in the terror. On the other hand, those family histories did not determine the politics of Perestroika. Ligachev soon became Gorbachev's leading opponent in the Communist Party; Shevardnadze resigned; and Yeltsin later destroyed Gorbachev's leadership.

In the end, Gorbachev's anti-Stalinist policies, for all their other ramifications, provided little material relief to surviving terror-era zeks. Some of their confiscated property was finally returned. The dacha Vyshinsky took from the condemned Serebryakov in 1937, for example, which had been occupied after Vyshinsky's death by several top officials, including Prime Minister Aleksei Kosygin, was given to the victim's elderly daughter thirty years after she returned from the Gulag in the 1950s. A few small possessions, as I mentioned earlier, were sent anonymously to families rehabilitated under Gorbachev.

But despite all the attention and promises Gorbachev's policies bestowed on Stalin's victims, many survivors remained so destitute in 1990 that one of their organizations issued a "SOS from the Gulag" pleading for private donations.[43] Bankrupt and crumbling politically, Gorbachev's government was never able to provide most of the social benefits it had legislated. And in December 1991, the state that had raised, arrested, and then liberated Stalin's victims ceased to exist. Almost all of the Gulag survivors I knew regretted its passing.

Anna Larina and the author at the Museum of the Revolution exhibit in 1988 marking Bukharin's official exoneration, the fiftieth anniversary of his execution, and the hundredth anniversary of his birth.

Above, Yuri Larin's first major exhibit in Russia, at the Tretyakov Exhibition Hall, 1989. From right to left: Anton Antonov-Ovseyenko; Leonid Petrovsky; Yuri; Giuliano Gramsci, son of the famous Italian Marxist; Yuri's son Kolya; the author; and Robert C. Tucker, the author's Indiana University professor and Princeton colleague. Below, Katrina with Anton and Leonid, at the same exhibit.

Above, from left to right: the playwright Mikhail Shatrov; the author; Anna Larina; Inge Ballod, Yuri Larin's wife, who died in 1987; and Yuri, at Shatrov's apartment, 1985. Below, the author and Katrina with the novelist Julian Semyonov at his apartment, 1985.

Aleksandr ("Sasha") Milchakov pointing out the terror-era mass grave at Donskoi Cemetery, 1989.

The author at an anti-Stalinist event in a Moscow park, 1989. The banner reads: "Put Stalinism on Trial of Public Opinion!"

Above, the author, his son Andrew, and Andrew's future wife, Sandra Tsang, on Red Square, May Day 1989, following the author's remarks on Soviet national television. Below, and in front of a poster announcing his appearance at an event during a "Week of Conscience," 1989.

The first public event honoring Khrushchev since his overthrow, 1989. Above and below, left to right: the author; Anna Larina; Roy Medvedev; and William vanden Heuvel, a Kennedy administration official when Khrushchev was Soviet leader and Katrina's father. (Photo below credit: Pyotr Krimerman)

Katrina, holding two-month-old Nika, between Anna Larina and
Yuri. Standing, from left to right: Eka; the author; Nadya; and Olga
Maksakova, Yuri's wife, 1991.

Anna Larina and Nika, 1995.

Above, Lev Razgon; Nika; and Galina Shevelyova, a family friend, 1992. Bottom right, the author, Katrina, and Nika with Anton, at the Larina family dacha, 1999. Bottom left, Svetlana Gurvich-Bukharin with the author and Nika, 1993.

Lazar Kogan, soon to be Bukharin's NKVD interrogator in Lubyanka Prison, and Kogan's daughter Tatyana, early 1930s.

Kogan's daughter Tatyana with Anna Larina, 1993.

The author and Anna Larina with Mikhail Gorbachev at the Gorbachev Foundation, 1995.

Anna Larina's funeral, 1996. Front row, from left: Misha; Nadya; the author; Yuri; and Misha's wife Tonya. Kolya is standing behind Misha and Nadya. (Credit: *The Moscow Times*)

A commemorative service at an NKVD mass burial site discovered at Butovo, near Moscow, where Bukharin is thought to have been buried. His daughter Svetlana is standing in the front row, far left. (Courtesy of Emma Gurvich)

The author and Anton Antonov-Ovseyenko at Anton's State Museum of the History of the Gulag, 2009.

Stalin's Victims and Russia's Future

*The Leader is near. And again, together with millions of people
who await his advent, we repeat like an incantation: he is at
hand, he is near, he will return.*

—Russian Ultra-Nationalist, 1999

Can it really be him? Yes, Stalin is back.

—Russian Ultra-Nationalist, 2004

As I finish this book, twenty years after Soviet Communism
ended and almost sixty years after Stalin's death, his role in history
continues to polarize Russia. In surveys taken in 2009 and 2010,
when the controversy reemerged as a major political issue, many
Russians thought Stalin was a "cruel, inhuman tyrant" who "killed
millions of innocent people." Many others believed he was a "great
and wise leader" who "did not repress any honest citizens," or that
the number of victims was less important than his achievements.[1]

Why have disputes over Stalin's rule persisted and even
intensified in the twenty-first century? Explaining opposition to
Gorbachev's reforms, an anti-Stalinist Soviet journalist gave part
of the answer: "Just as you and I cannot jump out of our skin,

a nation cannot leap out of its history."² Stalinism was a large, formative, and traumatic chapter in Russia's modern history, and therefore still weighs heavily and divisively on the nation, much as slavery, a no less formative chapter in American history, did in the United States for many decades after its abolition.

But an equal if not larger part of the explanation is to be found in developments in Russia since the end of the Soviet Union. Western commentators usually attribute the revival of pro-Stalin sentiments to the outlook and policies of Vladimir Putin, the career KGB officer who became Russia's second post-Soviet president in 2000. In reality, the "Stalinist renaissance," as it is called in Moscow, began in the turbulent 1990s, under Boris Yeltsin, the first post-Soviet president, and it came not from above but from below.

Early during his decade in office, Yeltsin issued three decrees that went beyond Gorbachev in condemning Stalin's terror. One rehabilitated all citizens politically repressed after 1917, not just those under Stalin. Another finally recognized the millions of children of arrested parents as victims, making them eligible for compensation as well.³ And the third declared an annual day of national mourning for Soviet political victims. In addition, Yeltsin passed a law giving victims and their families the right to examine their case files in the archives of the former NKVD.

For survivors who had the understanding, stamina, and financial means to gain access to the archives, it was a profound experience, as I witnessed on several occasions. In 1992, Anna Larina, her health failing, legally authorized me to examine Bukharin's prison records on her behalf. Studying those thick folders in Lubyanka's decrepit "reception" building in the center of Moscow, where desperate people had come in the 1930s in hope of obtaining news about arrested family members, I was deeply moved by the dozen or more elderly people bent over adjacent tables, their faces pressed close to the faded documents.

They turned the pages slowly, scrutinizing each false testimony and confession that had doomed their loved ones and sealed their own fates. Some said they were grateful for the chance to read the long-secret files, and returned day after day. Others were so upset they soon left and did not come back. Even Eugenia Ginzburg's son, the worldly author Vasily Aksyonov, was shaken by the experience: "Reading the archives of the Soviet secret police fills the soul with darkness and the body with lead. Especially if you are reading the 'case' of your own mother."[4]

Initially, Yeltsin's expanded policies favoring Stalin's victims were largely unchallenged. Graphic accounts of the terror appeared regularly on television. The Memorial Society, founded in Moscow in 1988, grew into a nation-wide organization exposing more mass executions and burial sites, lobbying Parliament for victims' rights, sponsoring commemorations at former Gulag camps across the country, and producing compelling studies of what had happened to so many innocent people. Another organization, Return, was formed to collect and publish memoirs of survivors. A full recognition of the dimensions of Stalin's terror and the undoing of his lingering reputation as a great leader seemed well under way.

The process was aborted by Yeltsin's decision to adopt the economic measures known as shock therapy. Introduced in the early 1990s to effect a rapid transition to free-market capitalism, they plunged post-Soviet Russia into an economic collapse greater than the American depression of the 1930s. While privatization turned the former Soviet state's most valuable financial assets over to Kremlin insiders, hyperinflation vaporized the value of salaries, pensions, and life savings. Some 75 percent of Russians fell into poverty, their traditional social entitlements vanished. Millions of homeless children suddenly appeared. The life expectancy of men dropped below sixty years. Official corruption and mafia-like crime swept the country.[5]

With the emergence of tens of millions of present-day victims, interest in those of a bygone era underwent a "catastrophic fall."[6] (When Anna Larina died in 1996, no member of the government or the Communist Party attended her funeral.) Meanwhile, Stalin's reputation rose on a tidal wave of social pain, anger, and nostalgia for Soviet times. Russia's diminished international standing enhanced his stature as the wartime leader who built a superpower. The emergence of two Russias, one suddenly rich and the other impoverished, made his austere economic policies seem like social justice. Flagrant unearned wealth and privilege recast his repressions as retribution against real enemies of the people.

Little of this rosy-tinted memory was historically true, but it was retrospective perceptions that mattered. In 1990, less than 10 percent of Russians surveyed had a positive opinion of Stalin's rule. A decade later, the number had tripled and, by 2005, had risen above 50 percent.[7] At the same time, favorable ratings of the two living anti-Stalinist leaders, Gorbachev and Yeltsin, along with Khrushchev's, fell into single digits. Popular support for their reforms since 1985, Soviet and post-Soviet, declined sharply.

In particular, the crises of the 1990s adversely affected the main political achievements of anti-Stalinists initiated by Gorbachev—Russia's democratization and historical truth-telling. Putin is usually blamed for reversing democratization, but the process actually began when Yeltsin used force to abolish an elected parliament in 1993, turned the mass media over to self-interested financial oligarchs, and in effect fixed his own reelection in 1996. Nor is it true, as Western journalists and academics assert, that Putin "shut down" the "investigation of Stalinist history."[8]

Instead, Putin's years in power have witnessed an open political struggle between resurgent neo-Stalinists and anti-Stalinists over the interpretation of the Soviet past. The battle has raged across the country, from St. Petersburg and Moscow to Arctic sites of the former Gulag, and in virtually every public forum: television, newspapers, books, schools, Parliament, political parties, and street demonstrations. Most Western accounts have focused only on the neo-Stalinists, without tracing their revived political fortunes to the Yeltsin 1990s.

Certainly, there has been a "Stalinist renaissance." Bookstore shelves have filled with glossy volumes extolling every aspect of Stalin's rule, including the terror. In these pages and those of Communist and ultra-nationalist newspapers, the "Rehabilitation of Stalin," as one series proudly declares, is complete.[9] On a special television program in 2008, he was chosen, after months of viewer voting, the third greatest Russian in history, behind an ancient warrior and a Tsarist minister.

Meanwhile, powerful forces have weighed in on the neo-Stalinist side. Putin's office promoted a textbook and teaching manuals sympathetic to Stalin's leadership in the 1930s. The KGB's successor, the FSB, moved against several anti-Stalinist projects, seizing their materials and briefly arresting at least one historian and harassing others. Symbols of the Stalin era began reappearing in public places, notably on the facade of a central Moscow subway, along with his image on well-made posters.

But anti-Stalinists have hardly been "shut down" under Putin. A popular newspaper, *Novaya Gazeta*, features a regular supplement, "Truth About the Gulag." Its pages are devoted to documents and commentaries about Stalin's "genocide," an ongoing "Trial of Stalin," and demands for a "new Nuremberg."[10] Dozens of historical studies and memoirs detailing the terror's impact on ordinary citizens as well as on revered institutions such as the army have been published, many of them cited in this book, as has a multi-volume *History of Stalinism* that includes translations of Western scholars.

The work of leading anti-Stalinist institutions has not been seriously hindered. The Gorbachev Foundation has held well-attended conferences on his anti-Stalinist predecessors, Khrushchev and Mikoyan, and on the terror itself. The Memorial Society continues to publicize mass graves, sponsor local "martyrologies," and lobby for the needs of survivors. Among its nationwide projects is a remarkable series of volumes of essays by high school students about the impact of Stalin's terror on their grandparents.[11]

Nor has anti-Stalinism been excluded from state-controlled television, the most important medium of Russian politics. Films based on books by Solzhenitsyn, Shalamov, Aksyonov, and other popular anti-Stalinist writers have been funded and broadcast to large audiences. Panel discussions of the Stalin era have included its outspoken critics. In 2009, the popular talk-show host Vladimir Pozner, for example, labeled Stalin "one of the worst villains in world history." In 2010, a new documentary based on Olga Shatunovskaya's investigations under Khrushchev, "The Nuremberg That Never Was," was being considered by television networks.[12]

As the example of state television indicates, anti-Stalinists, like their adversaries, have supporters in high places. Courts ordered the FSB to return materials it had seized and rejected a libel suit by Stalin's grandson against *Novaya Gazeta* for calling his grandfather a "blood-thirsty cannibal" and a "criminal." (The paper's lawyer heralded the decision as the "threshold of a Nuremberg trial of Stalinism.") Access to terror-era documents in some state archives tightened, but in others more have been declassified, including eighteen thousand in Magadan.[13] In 2008, members of Putin's own government participated in a Memorial Society conference on the Stalinist terror.

Moscow's mayor, Yuri Luzhkov, a powerful politician with ties to the Kremlin, is another indicative example. In 2002, he authorized a statue of the late writer and bard Bulat Okudzhava, a child of the terror and symbolic anti-Stalinist figure ever since Khrushchev's Thaw, in a revered cultural district. At the same time, Luzhkov turned over to Antonov-Ovseyenko valuable real estate in the center of Moscow, as well as operating funds, to found the first State Museum of the History of the Gulag, which opened in 2004.

In short, the political struggle over the Stalin era, which began under Khrushchev and figured so importantly in Gorbachev's reforms, resurfaced under Putin. As an anti-Stalinist remarked in 2007, the seventieth anniversary of the Great Terror, the underlying conflict between the "two Russias" observed by Anna Akhmatova in 1956 "has not been settled to this day." Once again it features a bitterly contested campaign to build a national memorial to Stalin's victims, first proposed by Khrushchev fifty years ago and now led by Gorbachev, the Memorial Society, and *Novaya Gazeta*.[14]

Putin's own role in the struggle has been contradictory. On occasions, he seemed to defend the entire Stalin era, perhaps as a way of reinforcing his own authoritarian policies. He repeatedly refused, for example, to criticize Stalin's conduct of the war against Germany, even the dictator's collaboration with Hitler on the eve of the Nazi invasion. Still more, Putin publicly endorsed a 2007 textbook that seemed to rationalize Stalin's extreme measures during the pre-war 1930s, including the terror, as a necessary form of "mobilization" for the "goals of modernization," while minimizing the number of victims.[15]

At other times, however, Putin has taken anti-Stalinist positions. Early in his presidency, he authorized an expanded investigation of Stalin-era crimes. In 2006, the FSB, which remained subordinate to him, honored a surviving victim, the well-known poet Naum Korzhavin. In 2007, Putin personally visited the ailing Solzhenitsyn, who still personified the Gulag fate of millions, presenting him with a state award. The same year, Putin attended a highly publicized commemoration of victims at a notorious NKVD killing field and burial site near Moscow, the first Kremlin leader ever to make such an appearance.[16]

There was more. When Solzhenitsyn died in 2008, Putin's government organized the equivalent of a state funeral, enacted measures to memorialize his life, and then made his *The Gulag Archipelago* mandatory reading in schools. In 2009, in the same vein, Putin told a national radio audience that Stalin-era achievements had involved "crimes against the nation that cannot be justified." In 2010, he invited Poland's prime minister to join him in a memorial service at Katyn, where Stalin's NKVD had infamously massacred thousands of Polish officers, again becoming the first Russian leader ever to attend such a commemoration.[17]

Putin's contradictory, or ambiguous, position on Stalin is not surprising. In the twentieth century, Russians had their Tsarist and Soviet histories officially repudiated as unworthy of respect. But no nation can flourish without at least a minimally consensual past to inspire it. Any twenty-first-century Russian leader will have to try to piece together such a past from fragments of the country's tragic history, as Putin has tried to do. The thirty-year Stalin era, with its heroic and costly victory over Nazi Germany and rise "from wooden plough to atomic bomb," cannot be entirely discarded. To do so, as even Gorbachev emphasized, would be "to renounce my own grandfather, my own father, and everything they did."[18]

By 2008, when Putin handed the presidency over to his protégé Dmitri Medvedev, while remaining preeminent as prime minister, the problem had become even larger, embracing not the only the past, but also the present and the future. Alarmed by the ongoing disintegration of the country's basic infrastructures, Russia's policy class and political intellectuals were engaged in an equally heated controversy over how to modernize the nation and what it meant. In this struggle for Russia's future, the Stalinist past and its conflicting lessons once again became a central issue.

For the Western-oriented side in the struggle, Russia's antiquated, near-total dependence on state-directed exports of natural resources, particularly energy, has to be replaced by a diversified, high-tech economy based on creative initiatives of its citizens. Therefore, a "successful modernization of the country is impossible without political democratization." Proponents of this approach and of this vision of Russia's future find only negative lessons in the nation's centuries-long tradition of state-imposed transformations, Stalin's being the most recent episode, which repeatedly resulted in semi-backward economies and an absence of individual freedom. For them, everything must begin with the "de-Stalinization of modernization."[19]

For the other side, on the contrary, the "optimal program for Russian modernization should consist of a kind of 'neo-Stalinism'—a concentration of resources under the state" with unlimited power "to eliminate all obstacles." Warning of the threat represented by the expansion of the West's military alliance, NATO, to Russia's borders, advocates of this "harsh system" equate the nation's future with an overweening state and unrivaled military power. Recalling Stalin's "salvation of the country" in the 1930s and 1940s, they maintain that "we can be saved only by civilized Stalinism."[20]

Readers can imagine the effect this resurgent neo-Stalinism, however "civilized," has had on surviving Gulag returnees. Indeed, the "Stalinist renaissance" has badly eroded the once "sacred" status of Stalin's victims, already overshadowed in politics and popular culture by Soviet victims of World War II and of post-Soviet economic shock therapy. Since the 1990s, legions of Gulag deniers have charged that anti-Stalinist studies of the terror era are "90 percent lies"; that few, if any, labor-camp zeks were "honest citizens"; that "rehabilitation euphoria" was a deceit; and that eminent victims, such as the geneticist Nikolai Vavilov, were not really more admirable than their victimizers.[21]

The dwindling number of Gulag survivors still alive in Russia is increasingly pessimistic. When I told Antonov-Ovseyenko I might title this book, *The Victims' Long Return*, he replied, thinking of his little-known museum, "It has been interrupted by

Stalin's long return." Grigory Pomerants, a philosopher and, like Anton, a very elderly former zek, warned, "False prophets tell us: You yourself are shit, but you are part of the glorious tradition of Aleksandr Nevsky and Joseph Stalin. And the day will come when the Russian Orthodox Church will canonize Stalin."[22]

Pomerants and my old friend Anton have good reason to worry. "Stalin is back," as his admirers happily proclaim,[23] not due to the design of a Kremlin leader but to the social pain and discontents that afflicted the nation after 1991. In response, most Russians blame anti-Stalinist reforms since the 1980s and want a "strong state" that will end the chaos and the pain. In this context, Stalin is a symbol of what they believe was once such a state and of their protests against today's official abuses and injustices. Very few Russians, as polls also show, actually want to live under a new Stalin.

Nor do the many ultra-nationalist politicians and ideologists who seize upon these popular sentiments and strive to delete the memory of Stalin's victims from Russia's present and future. The reconstituted Russian Communist Party, the second largest party after Putin's, for example, has reverted to a full-throated cult of Stalin while reviling as "pygmies" his opponents, from Khrushchev to Gorbachev, in its publications, ceremonies, and street rallies.[24] But the political and economic policies it actually proposes, in elections and in Parliament, are nothing like those of historical Stalinism.

Western commentators continue to blame pro-Stalin attitudes in Russia on the Kremlin's failure to fully condemn his crimes—though Gorbachev and Yeltsin did so—and to properly memorialize his victims. Readers know where my sympathies lie, but Americans should avoid such judgments. The U.S. House of Representatives and Senate issued formal apologies for slavery only in 2008 and 2009 respectively, a century and a half after it ended. No American president or full Congress has ever done so. Nor is there a U.S. national memorial to the millions of black people who lived and died as slaves—or anything like the hundreds of small local memorials to Stalin's victims across Russia today.

Nations whose histories include both greatness and great crimes, "majesty and misery," as a Russian poet characterized the Stalin era, cannot easily, it seems, find ways to reconcile the two. (Unfavorable comparisons of Russia with post-Hitler Germany are incorrect because de-Nazification was initially imposed on that defeated country by occupying forces.) Generations have to pass and conflicting memories dim before a national consensus can develop. Meanwhile, the struggle over the past, present, and future goes on, both sides rising, falling, and rising again.

In today's Russia, anti-Stalinism may seem to be losing the struggle in officialdom and in society, but, as readers know, it is a chapter in a much longer story. My perspective is the same as it was thirty years ago, before Gorbachev came to power, when Western specialists believed that anti-Stalinists had no political chance in the Soviet Union. As I argued then, because there is no political statute of limitations for historical crimes as massive, or of such "biblical dimensions," as those of the Stalin era,[25] they are certain to reemerge as a major factor in Russian politics, for at least two reasons.

First, even though most of Stalin's victims, including those who returned from the Gulag, are now dead, Russia remains a country significantly populated by their direct descendents, particularly their grandchildren. A few made their voices heard under Gorbachev, and many more are speaking out now. (Of Russians polled in 2006, 27 percent said their relatives had been repressed under Stalin.) Reverence for ancestors is a Russian tradition, so it is unlikely descendants of Stalin's victims will permit the nation to forget theirs. (With this in mind, Kamil Ikramov reflected, just before he died, on the "wonderful children and grandchildren left behind by those who perished.")[26]

Second, political leadership for a renewed reckoning with the crimes of the Stalin era is likely to come from the generation that came of age during Gorbachev's glasnost revelations, much as "children" of Khrushchev's Twentieth Party Congress, including Gorbachev himself, provided it in the fateful late 1980s. Indeed, the new Russian president, Dmitri Medvedev, who is thirteen years younger than Putin and has acknowledged having been influenced by Gorbachev's historical disclosures, has already moved in that direction.

In 2009, Medvedev intervened personally in the growing controversies over the Stalinist past. In February, he invited Gorbachev and the editor of *Novaya Gazeta*, Dmitri Muratov, to the Kremlin, using the occasion to publicly endorse "unconditionally" their campaign for a national memorial to Stalin's victims. Eight months later, Medvedev went further, expressing alarm that young Russians did not know about "the dimensions of the terror . . . about the millions of maimed lives. About the people shot without trial or investigation, about those dispatched to camps and exile . . . Millions of people perished as a result of the terror . . . Millions."[27]

Medvedev then took an equally unambiguous stand in the struggle over Russia's modernization and future. Insisting that "the memory of national tragedies is as sacred as the memory of victories," and rejecting the neo-Stalinist "justification of those who destroyed our people," he went on: "Even today we can hear that these countless victims were warranted by some higher state goals. I am convinced that no national development, successes, or goals can be achieved at the price of human grief or loss." For emphasis, Medvedev urged that the search for mass graves and the names of all the victims continue, and called for "memorial-museum centers that will pass the memory of what happened from generation to generation."

Clearly, the political struggle over the crimes of the Stalin era is again under way in Russia at the highest levels. It will almost certainly intensify. If so, the long return of the victims is not over.

A Few Words of Gratitude

Most of the people who made this book possible, survivors of Stalin's terror I first met more than thirty years ago, are no longer alive. In the hope that what I have written acknowledges their contributions, I will not name them again here, with one exception. *The Victims Return* is dedicated to the memory of Anna Larina because I could not have written it without her and because our twenty-year friendship enriched my life in so many other ways as well.

Happily, I will at long last be able to give this book to a few of Stalin's victims who helped me from the very beginning. Readers also know their names and contributions: Roy Medvedev, Anton Antonov-Ovseyenko, Tanya Bayeva, Leonid Petrovsky, and, of course, Anna Larina's children—Yuri Larin, Nadya Fadeyeva, and Misha Fadeyev.

Over the years, other Russian friends and colleagues also gave me valuable assistance, particularly Gennady Bordyugov, Irina Davidian, and the families of Svetlana Gurvich, Vladimir Bukharin, and Olga Shatunovskaya. More recently, Alexandra Aikhenvald, Yuri Aikhenvald's daughter and an eminent professor of linguistics, shared with me her special knowledge of her father's life and the lives of other Gulag returnees she knew.

The photographs and illustrations are an integral part of this book, and here too I am grateful to a number of people. They are acknowledged in the captions, but I want to thank again Alexandra Aikhenvald, Emma Gurvich, and the relatives of Olga Shatunovskaya for permission to use their family photographs; Aleksei Soldatenkov for the right to reprint the painting by his father, Igor Soldatenkov, that appears on the cover; and, far from least, my friend David King for letting me borrow from his unique photographic histories of the terror, *The Commissar Vanishes* and *Ordinary Citizens.* All of the other photographs, unless otherwise indicated, are from my own collection.

I had valuable help from fellow Americans as well. As readers will recall, conversations with Robert Conquest initially inspired this undertaking, and Lynn Blair Cohen, then my wife, was with me when it first began in Moscow. I have called upon their knowledge and memory ever since. Nanci Adler, whose own work has been essential, remains a close colleague and dear friend. Jonathan Sanders, a historian and former colleague at CBS News, copied rare photographs and documents for me in Moscow. Omar Rubio prepared all of the photographs and illustrations for publication.

I owe an especially large debt of gratitude to my exceedingly smart, skilled, and resourceful assistant, Arina Chesnokova, whose part in the latter stages of my work was indispensable. Having no knowledge of the Internet, or even a computer, I relied on her for many essential things, from research, fact-checking, acquiring documents and photographs, and correspondence to preparing the several drafts of the manuscript.

Above all, though, this book would not exist without the vital contributions of my fellow traveler and wife of many years, Katrina vanden Heuvel. Early on, when we spent time with victims together in Moscow, her questions, insights, and notes formed the basis of much that is now in the book. Later, I relied very heavily on her judgment about people, events, and how best to express what I wanted to write. For all of that, and much more, I am hugely, and lovingly, grateful.

S.F.C.
Moscow–New York
1976-2010

Notes

For the benefit of general readers, I have omitted from the endnotes a considerable number of non-essential sources, especially ones in Russian. Specialists who want to consult those additional sources will find many of them in the shorter, Russian-language version of this book: Stiven Koen, *Dolgoe vozvrashchenie: zhertvy GULAGa posle Stalina* (Moscow: AIRO XXI, 2009), cited here as Koen, *Dolgoe.*

Making this book fully accessible to general readers is also why the spelling of Russian names sometimes varies. In the text and often in the endnotes, I use the form most familiar to non-specialists—for example, Tatyana Bayeva, not Tatiana Baeva; Yevgeny Yevtushenko, not Evgenii Evtushenko; and Shatunovskaya, not Shatunovskaia. When I do cite Russian-language sources, however, I usually use the Library of Congress system of transliteration (though without hard and soft signs), which specialists prefer.

Prologue

1.   Andrei Timofeev in *Literaturnaia gazeta*, Aug. 23, 1995; and Mark Iunge and Rolf Binner, *Kak terror stal bolshim* (Moscow, 2003). The indispensable book on all of these events is Robert Conquest, *The Great Terror*, 40ᵗʰ anniversary ed. (New York, 2008).

2.   "Pravda GULAGa," *Novaia gazeta*, July 22, 2009.

3.   Quoted in Vitaly Shentalinsky, *Arrested Voices* (New York, 1996), 25–26, though I have modified the translation.

4.   For sexual abuse and beatings after sentencing, see A.G. Tepliakov, *Protsedura* (Moscow, 2007), 71–76. For Blyukher, husbands, wives, children, and rape, see, respectively, A.I. Kartunova in *Novaia i noveishaia istoriia*, no. 1 (2004): 182–83; V.B. Konasov and A.L. Kuzminykh in *Rossiiskaia istoriia*, no. 1 (2009): 117; Kamil Ikramov, *Delo moego ottsa* (Moscow, 1991), 119; and Conquest, *The Great Terror*, 127. For a special torture prison, see Lidiia Golovkova, *Sukhanovskaia tiurma* (Moscow, 2009).

5.   Svetlana Alliluyeva, *Twenty Letters to a Friend* (New York, 1967), 140.

Chapter 1

1.   See Anna Larina, *This I Cannot Forget: The Memoirs of Nikolai Bukharin's Widow* (New York, 1993).

2.   For my book, see Stephen F. Cohen, *Bukharin and the Bolshevik Revolution* (New York, 1973 and 1980).

3.   For a discussion, see Stephen F. Cohen, *Rethinking the Soviet Experience* (New York, 1985), especially chaps. 1, 3–5.

4.   There was, however, a narrow but useful doctoral dissertation: Jane P. Shapiro, "Rehabilitation Policy and Political Conflict in the Soviet Union" (Columbia University, 1967).

5. Aleksandr Solzhenitsyn, *The Gulag Archipelago*, vol. 3 (New York, 1976): 445–68.

6. For Gulag literature at the time, see Libushe Zorin, *Soviet Prisons and Concentration Camps: An Annotated Bibliography* (Newtonville, 1980). For Americans and the terror, see Tim Tzoulidis, *The Forsaken* (New York, 2008); and for a very informative memoir, Victor Herman, *Coming Out of the Ice* (New York, 1979).

7. See, e.g., Dariusz Tolczyk, *See No Evil* (New Haven, 1999), xix–xx, chaps. 4–5; and Leona Toker, *Return From the Archipelago* (Bloomington, IN, 2000), 49–52, 73. For Shalamov, see his letter to Solzhenitsyn in *Nezavisimaia gazeta*, April 9, 1998.

8. They included *Sibirskie ogni*, *Baikal*, *Prostor*, *Angara*, *Ural*, *Poliarnaia zvezda*, *Na rubezhe*, and *Dalnii vostok*.

9. Radio Liberty in Munich maintained an ongoing catalogue, *Arkhiv samizdata*.

10. See Stephen F. Cohen, ed., *An End to Silence* (New York, 1982), 7–14; and A. Antonov-Ovseenko, *Vragi naroda* (Moscow, 1996), 367.

11. For our relationship, see our conversation in *Novaia i noveishaia istoriia*, no. 2 (2006): 94–101; and Cohen, ed., *An End*.

12. Academician Bayev felt free to tell his story only many years later. See A.D. Mirzabekov, ed., *Akademik Aleksandr Baev* (Moscow, 1997), chap. 1.

13. Published in *Moskovskii komsomolets*, July 13, 1966, and translated here by George Shriver. For other tributes to Gnedin, see Evgenii Gnedin, *Vykhod iz labirinta* (Moscow, 1994); and Stephen F. Cohen, *Sovieticus*, exp. ed. (New York, 1986), 104–107. For Ikramov, see Aleksandr Proskurin, ed., *Vozvrashchennye imena*, 2 vols. (Moscow, 1989), vol.1: 208–09.

14. See, respectively, *Gulag Archipelago*; *Let History Judge* (New York, 1972); and *The Time of Stalin* (New York, 1981). For Solzhenitsyn's often contentious relations with other zeks after the Gulag, see Liudmila Saraskina, *Aleksandr Solzhenitsyn* (Moscow, 2008), parts 5–6; and for Medvedev's warm relations, his account in *Podem*, nos. 7 and 9 (1990).

15. They represented, that is, no more than about 30 percent of the total victims. See earlier, Prologue, n. 1.

16.   Several questionnaires were prepared after 1985. See *Gorizont*, no. 7 (1989): 63–64; Nanci Adler, *The Gulag Survivor* (New Brunswick, 2002), 121; *Moskvichi v GULAGe* (Moscow, 1996), 51–2; and Orlando Figes, *The Whisperers* (New York, 2007), 662.

17.   Saraskina, *Aleksandr Solzhenitsyn*, 553; and Reshetovskaya's memoirs mentioned earlier. Solzhenitsyn named his sources only many years later in *Arkhipelag Gulag*, vol. 1 (Moscow, 2008): 13–18. Figes's *The Whisperers* is based on many more cases than I had, and admirably so, but it was researched when surreptitiousness was no longer necessary and with teams of assistants across Russia. See pages 657–65.

18.   The report was published many years later in *Literaturnaia gazeta*, no. 27 (1996).

19.   Cohen, ed., *An End*, a volume based on Roy Medvedev's *samizdat* materials; and Cohen, *Rethinking*.

20.   Adler, *Gulag Survivor*.

21.   Introduction to A. Antonov-Ovseenko, *Portret tirana* (Moscow, 1995), 3.

22.   Anne Applebaum, *Gulag* (New York, 2003), 515.

23.   See Raisa Orlova and Lev Kopelev, *My zhili v Moskve* (Moscow, 1990); and Kersnovskaia, *Skolko stoit chelovek* (Moscow, 2006). For other recent memoirs, see Anna Tumanova, *Shag vpravo, shag vlevo . . .* (Moscow, 1995); Aleksandr Milchakov, *Molodost svetlaia i tragicheskaia* (Moscow, 1988); Pavel Negretov, *Vse dorogi vedut na Vorkutu* (Benson, VT, 1985); Anatolii Zhigulin, *Chernye kamni* (Moscow, 1989); Mikhail Mindlin, *Anfas i profil* (Moscow, 1999); Olga Shatunovskaia, *Ob ushedshem veke* (La Jolla, CA, 2001); and Nadezhda Ulanovskaia and Maia Ulanovskaia, *Istoriia odnoi semi* (St. Petersburg, 2005). Most still focus, however, on life in the Gulag, as do, e.g., those in Simeon Vilensky, ed., *Till My Tale Is Told* (Bloomington, IN, 1999). For general Western studies, see earlier, nn. 7, 22; Adam Hochschild, *The Unquiet Ghost* (New York, 1994); Simon Sebag Montefiore, *Stalin* (London, 2003); Kathleen E. Smith, *Remembering Stalin's Victims* (Ithaca, 1996); Catherine Merridale, *Night of Stone* (New York, 2001); and Figes, *The Whisperers*.

24.   Partial exceptions are Miriam Dobson, *Khrushchev's Cold Summer: Gulag Returnees, Crimes, and The Fate of Reform after Stalin* (Ithaca,

2009); and N.F. Bugai, *Reabilitatsiia repressirovannykh grazhdan Rossii* (Moscow, 2006), which focuses primarily on repressed nationalities, not on individuals. Adler continues her research; a conference on the Gulag held at Harvard University in 2006 may result in publications on returnees; Kathleen E. Smith is preparing a book on 1956 dealing extensively with returning zeks; and Figes, *The Whisperers*, chap. 8, though over-generalizing, is a valuable contribution, as are those sections of Merridale's *Night of Stone* that treat the general theme. There are still only a few pages on the subject in Russian literature, as in Elena Zubkova, *Russia After the War* (Armonk, 1998), chap. 16; and *Mir posle Gulaga* (St. Petersburg, 2004). For archive volumes, see *Reabilitatsiia*, 3 vols. (Moscow, 2000–04) and *Deti GULAGa* (Moscow, 2002). Bukharin's relatives are among the best documented returnee cases. See Larina, *This I Cannot Forget*; Mark Iunge, *Strakh pered proshlym* (Moscow, 2003); V.I. Bukharin, *Dni i gody* (Moscow, 2003); A.S. Namazova, ed., *Rossiia i Evropa*, no. 4 (Moscow, 2007): 190–296 (on Bukharin's daughter, Svetlana Gurvich); and my introduction to Bukharin's prison novel, *How It All Began* (New York, 1998).

Chapter 2

1.   Razgon also learned what Stalin's respiration meant. See *True Stories*, 245. For Ikramov, see his *Delo*, 166.

2.   Aleksandr Proshkin in *Sovetskaia kultura*, June 30, 1988.

3.   On issues of survival, see, e.g., Varlam Shalamov *Kolyma Tales* and *Graphite* (New York, 1980 and 1981); Eugenia Ginzburg, *Within the Whirlwind* (New York, 1981); Nadezhda Mandelstam, *Hope Against Hope* (New York, 1970), 178; and Razgon, *True Stories*, 7.

4.   Tomasz Kizny, *Gulag* (Buffalo, NY, 2004), 289.

5.   For an illustrated study of the practice, see David King, *The Commissar Vanishes* (New York, 1997).

6.   See A.B. Suslov in *Voprosy istorii*, no. 3 (2004): 125; and *Istoriia stalinskogo GULAGa*, 7 vols. (Moscow, 2004–05), vol. 5: 90.

7.   Emma Gershtein, *Moscow Memoirs* (New York, 2004), 456.

8.   Josephine Wohl, *Invented Truths* (Durham, 1991), 22; Anatolii Rybakov in *Knizhnoe obozrenie*, no. 45 (1995): 10. For a few of many examples, see *Deti GULAGa*; Pyotr Yakir, *A Childhood in Prison*, (New York , 1973); Ikramov, *Delo*; Inna Shikheeva-Gaister, *Semeinaia khronika vremen kulta lichnosti* (Moscow, 1998); *Kak nashikh dedov zabirali* (Moscow, 2007); and Owen Matthews, *Stalin's Children* (New York, 2008). For a young suicide, see Zoia Eroshok in *Novaia gazeta*, Oct. 7, 2009.

9.   See A. Iu. Gorcheva, *Pressa Gulaga* (Moscow, 2009), 90–95; and, more generally, Cathy A. Frierson and Semyon S. Vilensky, *Children of the Gulag* (New Haven, 2010).

10.   Matthews, *Stalin's Children*, 75, 100. For Yuri, see Ikramov, *Delo*, 148.

11.   "Pravda GULAGa," *Novaia gazeta*, Oct. 30, 2008. Similarly, see Frierson and Vilensky, *Children*, 312–14.

12.   "Spoiled biographies"—people "whose fates were ruined by political repression" (Aleksei Karpychev in *Rossiiskie vesti*, March 28, 1995)—run through Figes, *The Whisperers*. For Pyotr Petrovky's widow, see *Golosa istorii*, no. 22, book 1 (Moscow, 1990): 230.

13.   See Olga Aroseva and Vera Maksimova, *Bez grima* (Moscow, 2003); *I, Maya Plisetskaya* (New Haven, 2001); Boris Efimov, *Moi desiat desiatiletii* (Moscow, 2000), and for Ilya Ehrenburg's doubts, Boris Frezinskii, *Pisateli i sovetskie vozhdi* (Moscow, 2008), 201; and Vladimir Molchanov in *Politicheskii klass*, Oct. 14, 2008. For Netto, see Lev Lure and Irina Maliarova, *1956 god* (St. Petersburg, 2007), 214; and, more generally, Robert Edelman, *Spartak Moscow* (Ithaca, 2009).

14.   Peter Pringle, *The Murder of Nikolai Vavilov* (New York, 2008), 250, 282. For the rest of my account, see Iurii Vavilov, *V dolgom poiske* (Moscow, 2004); and Vladimir Shaikin, *Nikolai Vavilov* (Moscow, 2006), 211–14.

15.   For Maretskaya's story, see T. Iakovleva in *Komsomolskaia pravda*, July 12, 1989; and her family website (maretski.ru).

16.   Aleksei Novikov in *Rossiiskie vesti*, March 28, 1995.

17. *Novyi mir*, no. 6 (1988): 106.

18. See Golfo Alexopoulos in *Slavic Review*, Summer 2005.

19. See, e.g., the correspondence between Gerstein, Gumilyov, and Akhmatova in Gerstein, *Moscow Memoirs*, 448–70.

20. Nikita Petrov, *Pervyi predsedatel KGB: Ivan Serov* (Moscow, 2005); and Ikramov, *Delo*, 59.

21. Aleksandr Zviagintsev, *Rudenko* (Moscow, 2008), chaps. 3–8.

22. See, respectively, Matthews, *Stalin's Children*, 115; and Kopelev, *Ease My Sorrows* (New York, 1983), 218.

23. See Milchakov, *Molodost*; Shatunovskaia, *Ob ushedshem*; Yakir, *Childhood*; and, for other examples, Koen, *Dolgoe*, 86.

24. Tatiana Okunevskaia, *Tatianin den* (Moscow, 1998), 411, 435–38; Victoria Fyodorova and Haskel Frankel, *The Admiral's Daughter* (New York, 1979); S. Frederick Starr, *Red and Hot* (New York, 1983), 194–257; Montefiore, *Stalin*, 396–99; and Koen, *Dolgoe*, 87. For the Starostins, see Edelman, *Spartak*.

25. Larissa Vasilieva, *Kremlin Wives* (New York, 1994), 155–59.

26. *Reabilitatsiia*, vol. 1: 213. For the slow process, see the posthumous case of Meyerhold in B. Riazhskii, "Kak shla reabilitatsiia," *Teatralnaia zhizn*, no. 5 (1989): 8–11. For the period, see Adler, *Gulag Survivor*, chap. 3.

27. Ibid., 89, 104. For the crowds, see Riazhskii, "Kak shla," 10; for the appeals, Shatunovskaia, *Ob ushedshem*, 431, and Antonov-Ovseenko, *Portret*, 452.

28. Gerstein, *Moscow Memoirs*, 464.

29. See Masha Gessen, *Ester and Ruzua* (New York, 2004), 307; Naum Korzhavin, *V soblaznakh krovavoi epokhi*, vol. 2 (Moscow, 2006): 704; for the decision to read the speech publicly, *Izvestiia TsK KPSS*, no. 3 (1989): 166; and, similarly, Koen, *Dolgoe*, 87.

30. Shatunovskaia, *Ob ushedshem*, 286–87.

31. P.E. Shelest, . . . *Da ne sudimy budete* (Moscow, 1995), 113–15. Sources on the commissions vary somewhat in their details. See Koen, *Dolgoe*, 88.

32. Vadim Tumanov, *"Vse poteriat—i vnov nachat s mechty"* (Moscow, 2004),168–71. Similarly, see Moris Gershman, *Prikliucheniia amerikantsa v Rossii* (New York, 1995), 254–56; and Koen, *Dolgoe*, 88.

33. V.N. Zemskov in *Sotsiologicheskie issledovaniia*, no. 7 (1991): 14. For the commission numbers, see Koen, *Dolgoe*, 88.

34. For the descriptions in this and the preceding paragraph, see Grigori Svirski, *A History of Post-War Soviet Writing* (Ann Arbor, 1981), 101; Tzoulidis, *The Forsaken*, 37; Shatunovskaia, *Ob ushedshem*, 282; and, similarly, Koen, *Dolgoe*, 88.

35. Nikolay Zabolotsky, *Selected Poems* (Manchester, UK, 1999), 190; Grossman, *Everything Flows* (New York, 2009), 75–76; and, similarly, L.A. Voznesenskii, *Istiny radi* (Moscow, 2004), 686.

36. *Gulag*, vol. 3: 470.

37. Negretov, *Vse dorogi*. Similarly, see Adler, *Gulag Survivor*, 231–33; and Koen, *Dolgoe*, 88.

38. See, e.g. Hochschild, *Unquiet Ghost*; Colin Thubron, *In Siberia* (New York, 1999), 38–48; and for skulls, Yevgeny Yevtushenko in *Literaturnaia gazeta*, Nov. 2, 1988.

39. Cohen, ed., *An End*, 66–67.

Chapter 3

1. Applebaum, *Gulag*, 512.

2. Mikhail Ardov, Boris Ardov, Aleksei Batalov, and Iurii Arpishkin, *Legendarnaia Ordynka* (Moscow , 1995), 101. For other examples of long lives, see Koen, *Dolgoe*, 89.

3. See, respectively, Grossman, *Everything Flows*, 93; Orlova and Kopelev, *My zhili*, 347–48; and Svirski, *A History*, 197.

4. See, respectively, Oleg Khlebnikov on Shalamov in *Novaia gazeta*, June 18–20, 2007; Gerstein, *Moscow Memoirs*, 423; Lure and Maliarova, *1956 god*, 281; Aleksei Snegov at a closed meeting of Party historians in 1956; the obituary of Valentin Zeka (Sokolov) in *Russkaia mysl*, Dec. 20,

1984; Saraskina, *Aleksandr Solzhenitsyn*, 456; and Iu. Iziumov in *Dose*, May 29, 2003. For other examples, see Koen, *Dolgoe*, 89.

5.   See Mirzabekov, ed., *Akademik*, chap. 1; and for similar professional conduct, Tumanova, *Shag*, 213–26.

6.   B.M. Firsov, *Raznomyslie v SSSR* (St. Petersburg, 2008), 123; and for Rokossovsky, Rodric Braithwaite, *Moscow 1941* (New York, 2007), 38–40.

7.   *Istoricheskii arkhiv*, no. 2 (2008): 30–41; N. Koroleva, *Otets*, vol. 2 (Moscow, 2006).

8.   Natalia Sats, *Zhizn—iavlenie polosatoe* (Moscow, 1991), 353–56; Larina, *This I Cannot Forget*, 233.

9.   Aikhenvald died in 1993. His last published book, *Poslednie stranitsy* (Moscow, 2003), contains an autobiography, poems, and essays.

10.   E.P. Vittenburg, *Pavel Vittenburg* (St. Petersburg, 2003); and for Sef, *Literaturnaia gazeta*, Oct. 22–28, 2008.

11.   For examples of happy and unhappy ends, see Adler, *Gulag Survivor*; Figes, *The Whisperers*; and Koen, *Dolgoe*, 90. For Ikramov, see *Delo*, 56,147.

12.   For Shalamov, see John Glad in Shalamov, *Graphite*, 9; and Elena Zakharova in *Novaia gazeta*, Nov. 8–11, 2007. For Berggolts, see Gerbert Kemoklidze in *Literaturnaia gazeta*, Nov. 12–18, 2008; and Daniil Granin, *Prichudy moei pamiati* (St. Petersburg, 2008), 104–06.

13.   *Reabilitatsiia*, vol. 2: 351. For first-hand accounts of Communist returnees, see Orlova and Kopelev, *My zhili*: and Ulanovskaia and Ulanovskaia, *Istoriia*; and for scholarly studies, Adler, *Gulag Survivor*, 29, 205–23, and Dobson, *Khrushchev's Cold Summer*, especially pages 69–77. Adler is completing a book on returnee attitudes toward the Party. A chapter appeared in *Europe-Asia Studies*, March 2010, 211–34.

14.   Ulanovskaia and Ulanovskaia, *Istoriia*, 267.

15.   *Nikita Sergeevich Khrushchev: dva tsveta vremeni*, 2 vols. (Moscow, 2009), vol. 2: 572–73.

16.   I am grateful to Nanci Adler for this quote.

17. For the father and son, see Olga Semenova, *Iulian Semenov* (Moscow, 2006).

18. Solzhenitsyn in *Novyi mir*, no. 4 (1999): 163. For Shalamov, see Svetlana Boym in *Slavic Review*, Summer 2008: 347; Zinovy Zink in *The Times Literary Supplement*, Dec. 5, 2008: 6; and, similarly, Koen, *Dolgoe*, 90.

19. See, respectively, Iurii Kariakin, *Peremena ubezhdeniia* (Moscow, 2007), 232; Ginzburg, *Within*, 390; and the viewpoints in Antonov-Ovseenko, *Portret*, 469–77, and Smith, *Remembering*, 177–78.

20. See Karpov in *Sovetskaia Rossiia*, July 27, 2002, *Pravda*, April 26, 1995, and his *Generalissimus*, 2 vols. (Moscow, 2002); Sviashchennik Dmitrii Dudko, *Posmertnye vstrechi so Stalinym* (Moscow, 1993); and Rokossovsky quoted in *Sovetskaia Rossiia*, March 6, 2008, and in *Molotov Remembers* (Chicago, 1933), 290.

21. A.L. Litvin, ed., *Dva sledstvennykh dela E. Ginzburg* (Kazan, 1994), 14.

22. See, respectively, Razgon, *True Stories*, 269; Mandelstam, *Hope Against Hope*, 377; Kersnovskaia, *Skolko stoit*, 347; Aroseva, *Bez grima*, 89; and *Reabilitirovan posmertno*, 2 vols. (Moscow, 1988), vol. 1: 104–06.

23. Aroseva, *Bez grima*, 88–89, 255.

24. See, e.g. Frierson and Vilensky, *Children*, 362–64; and the report by Anna Arutunyan in *Moscow News*, Nov. 16, 2009.

25. Vasilii Aksenov, *Zenitsa oka* (Moscow, 2005), 399–410; Orlova and Kopelev, *My zhili*, 359; Elena Bonner, *Mothers and Daughters* (New York, 1993), 328–33.

26. See Koen, *Dolgoe*, 91; and T.I. Shmidt, *Dom na naberezhnoi* (Moscow, 2009), 27.

27. Matthews, *Stalin's Children*, 105–08; Donald J. Raleigh, ed., *Russia's Sputnik Generation* (Bloomington, IN, 2006), 168–74; Bonner, *Mothers*, 323; and, similarly, Shmidt, *Dom*, 84. For Okudzhava and this general theme, see Alexander Etkind in *The Russian Review*, Oct. 2009: 623–40.

28. Ginzburg, *Within*, 410-11; *Everything Flows*, 11. Similarly, see Koen, *Dolgoe*, 91.

29.   Irina Shcherbakova, ed., *Kak nashikh dedov zabirali* (Moscow, 2007), 502.

30.   Vilensky, ed., *Till My Tale*, 280, 284. For examples similar to Gnedin, see Milchakov, *Molodost*, 91–92; and Baitalsky, *Notebooks*, 389–91. For a contrary example, see Lakshin in *Literaturnaia gazeta*, Aug. 17, 1994; and, more generally, Adler, *Gulag Survivor*, 139–45.

31.   Shalamov, *Graphite*, 281.

32.   Mandelstam, *Hope Against Hope*, 279.

33.   Natalia Kozlova, *Sovetskie liudi* (Moscow, 2005), 345.

34.   Orlova and Kopelev, *My zhili*, 75; Michael Scammell, *Solzhenitsyn* (New York, 1984), 657.

35.   Svirski, *A History*, 183.

36.   Oleg Volkov, *Pogruzhenie vo tmu* (Moscow, 1992), 428–29.

37.   Vilensky, ed., *Till My Tale*, 98.

38.   For a discussion, see Adler, *Gulag Survivor*. For examples, circles, and nostalgia, see Koen, *Dolgoe*, 91–92.

39.   See Adler, *Gulag Survivor*, 186–90; for statutes, *Reabilitatsiia*, vol. 2: 181–83, 194–97, 333–34; and for examples, Adler, *Gulag Survivor*, 92 n. 67.

40.   *I, Maya Plisetskaya*, 39.

41.   Shentalinsky, *Arrested Voices*, 285.

42.   Yury Trifonov, *The Disappearance* (Ann Arbor, 1991), 67; and Shmidt, *Dom*, 92.

43.   See, e.g., Irina Shcherbakova, ed., *Krug semi i koleso istorii* (Moscow, 2008), 251.

44.   A.V. Antonov-Ovseenko, *Respublika Abkhaziia* (Moscow, 2008), 19–20.

45.   Arkady Vaksberg, *Stalin's Prosecutor* (New York, 1991), 86–93.

46.   E. Efimov in *Sotsialisticheskaia zakonnost*, no. 9 (1964): 42–45; and Lev Zaverin in *Soiuz*, no. 51 (1990): 9.

47.   See Adler, *Gulag Survivor*, chap. 5.

48.   For Leonid Petrovsky's later accounts of his grandparents, see *Voprosy istorii KPSS*, no. 2 (1988): 93–97; and *Rabotnitsa*, no. 3 (1988): 17–19.

49.   See Ryazhsky's memoir-account in *Teatralnaia zhizn*, no. 5 (1989): 8–11.

50.   Adler, *Gulag Survivor*, 171, 177; Ivan Zemlianushin in *Trud*, Dec. 24, 1992. The figures are probably compatible because the first refers to 1954–1961 and the second apparently to 1954–1964.

51.   See Adler, *Gulag Survivor*, 179; and, similarly, Moshe Zaltsman, *Menia reabilitirovali* (Moscow, 2006), 247. For the other quotes and examples, see Koen, *Dolgoe*, 93.

52.   For her story, see "Pravda GULAGa," *Novaia gazeta*, July 29, 2009; and for the other examples, Koen, *Dolgoe*, 93.

53.   For the reception, see Zaraev in *Ogonek*, no. 15 (1991): 15; Adler, *Gulag Survivor*, 186; and Korzhavin, *V soblaznakh*, vol. 2: 657. For examples of kindness, see Voznesenskii, *Istiny*, 678.

54.   *I, Maya Plisetskaya*, 34; on smoke, Mandelstam, *Hope Against Hope*, 33; and on the amnesty, Dobson, *Khrushchev's Cold Summer*, chaps. 1–6.

55.   Snegov in *Vsesoiuznoe soveshchanie istorikov* (Moscow, 1964), 270; and, similarly, Vladimir Amlinskii in *Iunost*, no. 3 (1988): 53.

56.   For these latter examples, see Koen, *Dolgoe*, 94. For teachers, orphans, mailed notes, the doctor, and Peshkova, see, respectively, Shmidt, *Dom*, 77–78; *Shatrov*, vol. 5 (Moscow, 2007): 383; *I, Maya Plisetskaya*, 41, and Mandelstam, *Hope Against Hope*, 345; "Pravda GULAGa," *Novaia gazeta*, Sept. 9, 2009; and Gorcheva, *Pressa Gulaga*, 171, 220.

57.   E.S. Levina, *Vavilov, Lysenko, Timofeev-Resovskii* (Moscow, 1995), 134–35. For other examples, see Koen, *Dolgoe*, 94.

58.   Lidiia Chukovskaia, *Zapiski ob Anne Akhmatovoi*, vol. 2 (Paris, 1980): 115, 137; and, similarly, Lev Razgon in *Literaturnaia gazeta*, Dec. 13, 1995.

59.   *True Stories*, 276.

60. Boris Rubin, *Moe okruzhenie* (Moscow, 1995), 187.

61. Aroseva, *Bez grima*, 255–64; and *Molotov Remembers*, 281.

62. Antonov-Ovseenko, *Vragi naroda*, 16. For Ikramov, see *Delo*, 171.

63. For the quotes in this and the preceding paragraph, see, respectively, *Istoricheskii arkhiv*, no. 1 (2008): 80; Svirski, *A History*, 53; and *Aleksandr Fadeev: pisma i dokumenty* (Moscow, 2001), 297–98.

64. For these and other examples, see Koen, *Dolgoe*, 95; and Mandelstam, *Hope Against Hope*, 48.

65. Dobson, *Khrushchev's Cold Summer*, 122; Svirski, *A History*, 353, 367; Ludmilla Alexeyeva and Paul Goldberg, *The Thaw Generation* (Boston, 1990), 84; and, similarly, Koen, *Dolgoe*, 96.

66. Quoted by Tseitlin in *Krokodil*, no. 7 (1989): 6.

67. Iurii Panov in *Izvestiia*, Aug. 10, 1990; and Viktor Bokarev in *Literaturnaia gazeta*, March 29, 1989.

68. See Kersnovskaia, *Skolko stoit*; and for other published volumes of Gulag art, Koen, *Dolgoe*, 96.

69. Konstantin Simonov in *Izvestiia*, Nov. 18, 1962. For examples of earlier works, see Koen, *Dolgoe*, 96–97.

70. See Alexander Yanov, *The Russian New Right* (Berkeley, 1978), 15; Dmitri Volkogonov, *Stalin*, 2 vols. (3rd ed., Moscow, 1992), vol. 2: 626; and Solzhenitsyn, *Oak*, 16.

Chapter 4

1. See, e.g., the complaints by Ivan Isaev in *Istoricheskii arkhiv*, no. 2 (2001): 123–24; and V. Ivanov-Paimen, ibid., no. 4 (2003): 23–24.

2. Saraskina, *Aleksandr Solzhenitsyn*, 523. For the directors, see Emily Tall in *Slavic Review*, Summer 1990: 184; and V. Loginov and N. Glovatskaia in *Voprosy ekonomiki*, no. 1 (2007): 154–56.

3. See Koen, *Dolgoe*, 97–98.

4. See, e.g., S.A. Mikoian, "Aleksei Snegov v borbe za destalinizatsiiu," *Voprosy istorii*, no. 4 (2006): 69–83; Sergei Khrushchev, *Khrushchev on Khrushchev* (Boston, 1990), chap. 1; the name index in *Reabilitatsiia*, vols. 1–3, and in K. Aimermakher, ed., *Doklad N.S. Khrushchev o kulte lichnosti Stalina na XX sezde KPSS* (Moscow, 2002); and for the writer, Firsov, *Raznomyslie*, 249.

5. Shatunovskaia, *Ob ushedshem*; and Grigorii Pomerants, *Sledstvie vedet katorzhanka* (Moscow, 2004). For the quote, see Pomerants, "Pamiati odinokoi teni," *Znamia*, no. 7 (2006): 165.

6. Anastas Mikoian, *Tak bylo* (Moscow, 1999), 589; and the accounts by the sons previously cited, n. 4.

7. For these events, see the sources previously cited, nn. 4–6.

8. Khrushchev, *Khrushchev*, 13; and, similarly, Mikoian, "Aleksei Snegov."

9. See, respectively, Milchakov, *Molodost*, 94–98; Dmitrii Shelestov, *Vremia Alekseia Rykova* (Moscow, 1990), 296; Dmitrii Bykov in *Rodina*, no. 8 (2008): 118–19; Bonner, *Mothers*, 323–24; A. Afanasev in *Komsomolskaia pravda*, Jan. 15, 1988; and, for more examples, Koen, *Dolgoe*, 99.

10. Nadezhda Ulanovskaia in *Vremia i my*, no. 77 (1983): 217–41; and Miklos Kun, *Stalin* (Budapest, 2003), 79. For a sympathetic biography, see M.Iu. Pavlov, *Anastas Mikoian* (Moscow, 2010).

11. Shatrov in *Svobodnaia mysl*, no. 10 (1994): 22; and for Molotov, *Istoricheskii arkhiv*, no. 3 (1993): 76.

12. See Saraskina, *Aleksandr Solzhenitsyn*, 480–98; for Khrushchev's own victim, Vladimir Semichastnyi, *Bespokoinoe serdtse* (Moscow, 2002), 79; and for Aksyonov, *Nikita Sergeevich Khrushchev*, vol. 2: 538–39.

13. William Taubman, *Khrushchev* (New York, 2002), 274–75, 276–77; Shatrov in *Svobodnaia mysl*, no. 10 (1994): 22; and *Nikita Khrushchev 1964* (Moscow, 2007), 442.

14. For the moral factor, see Roy Medvedev, *Khrushchev* (Garden City, NY, 1983), 87–91; Orlova and Kopelev, *My zhili*, 31; and, similarly, Koen, *Dolgoe*, 99–100. For Pomerants, see his "Pamiati," 166, and his *Sledstvie*, 138–39.

15. One returnee witness, Suren Gazaryan, wrote a memoir account of Beria's trial. See *SSSR: Vnutrennie protivorechiia* (New York), no. 6 (1982): 109–46.

16. For Lazurkina, see *XXII sezd kommunisticheskoi partii Sovetskogo Soiuza*, 3 vols. (Moscow, 1962), vol. 3: 121; and *Molotov Remembers*, 367.

17. Iurii Trifonov, *Otblesk kostra* (Moscow, 1966), 86.

18. See, respectively, Alliluyeva, *Twenty Letters*, 222; N.S. Khrushchev, *Vremia. Liudi. Vlast.*, 4 vols. (Moscow, 1999), vol. 2: 184; Viktor Danilov in *Kritika*, Spring 2008: 355; Georgii Ostroumov in *Proryv k svobode* (Moscow, 2005), 288; and, similarly, Alexeyeva and Goldberg, *The Thaw Generation*.

19. *The Time of Stalin*, xviii.

20. Frierson and Vilensky, *Children*, 365.

21. Anatolii Rybakov, *Roman-vospominanie* (Moscow, 1997), 84.

22. Oleg Litskevich in *Svobodnaia mysl*, no. 6 (2008): 135–44.

23. For these projects and their results, see Koen, *Dolgoe*, 101.

24. A recurring charge at a Central Committee meeting in 1957. See *Molotov, Malenkov, Kaganovich. 1957* (Moscow, 1998).

25. Vavilov, *V dolgom poiske*, 176.

26. *Ob ushedshem.*

27. Quoted in Medvedev, *Khrushchev*, 81. For "fashion," see Vladimir Lakshin in *Literaturnaia gazeta*, Aug. 17, 1994; and for Shatunovskaya, Pomerants, *Sledstvie*, 12.

28. For Serov, see Petrov, *Pervyi predsedatel*; and for archive documents, Koen, *Dolgoe*, 101–02.

29. N. Barsukov in *Kommunist*, no. 8 (1990): 99.

30. See Koen, *Dolgoe*, 103; and for the quote, Nikita Petrov in *Novoe vremia*, no. 23 (2000): 33.

31. *Molotov, Malenkov, Kaganovich.* Quotes and details cited here are from *Istoricheskii arkhiv*, no. 3 (1993): 17, 19, 85, 88.

32. Ibid., no. 4 (1993): 17.

33. See Koen, *Dolgoe*, 103; Petrov, *Pervyi predsedatel*, 151; and for total dismissals, Julie Elkner in Melanie Ilic and Jeremy Smith, eds., *Soviet State and Society Under Khrushchev* (London, 2009), 146.

34. Koen, *Dolgoe*, 103.

35. For Khrushchev, Serebryakova, Ikramov, Razgon, guards, and my publisher, see, respectively, Medvedev, *Khrushchev*, 97 (and, similarly, Shatunovskaia, *Ob ushedshem*, 286); *Khrushchev: dva tsveta*, vol. 2: 574; *Delo*, 168–69; *True Stories*, 235; Paul R. Gregory, *Lenin's Brain and Other Tales from the Secret Soviet Archives* (Stanford, CA, 2008), 91; and Aleksandr Avelichev in *Stephen Cohen, The Soviet Union and Russia* (Exeter, NH, 2010), 79–80.

36. For the estimates, the poet, and Khrushchev, see Dmitri Volkogonov in *Moscow Times Magazine*, Aug. 13, 1995: 21, and Galina Ivanova in *Obshchaia gazeta*, Aug. 27, 1998–Sept. 2, 1998; Pavel Antokolskii in *Grani*, no. 56 (1964): 182; and the first two citations in the preceding note. For a camp economic manager, see the forthcoming memoirs of Fyodor Mochulsky, *Gulag Boss*, edited by Deborah Kaple.

37. For obeying orders, see Piatnitskii, *Osip Piatnitskii*, 610–11; Mandelstam, *Hope Against Hope*, 49; and Tzouliadis, *The Forsaken*, 320. For archive documents implicating Khrushchev, see Koen, *Dolgoe*, 101–02.

38. Saraskina, *Aleksandr Solzhenitsyn*, 478. All quotes in this and the following paragraph are from the proceedings, *XXII sezd*, vol. 3: 121–22, 362, 402, 584. (For children, see page 114.)

39. *Ob ushedshem*, 297–300. For the commission's final report, see *Reabilitatsiia*, vol. 2: 541–670.

40. Vladimir Lakshin in *Novyi mir*, no. 1 (1964).

41. See, respectively, Boris Polevoi in *Ogonek*, July 1962: 20–24; V. Starikov in *Ural*, no. 4 (1963): 4–48; Ikramov in *Molodaia gvardiia*, no. 12 (1962): 183–234; and Aksyonov in *Iunost: izbrannye* (Moscow, 1965), 9–36.

42. *Den poezii 1962* (Moscow, 1962), 45. I remain grateful to the late Professor Vera Dunham, who brought this poem to my attention and translated it. For officials, see, e.g., Adler's discussion of Ivan Lazutin's novel, in *Gulag Survivor*, 179–81; and for generations, Ikramov in *Molodaia gvardiia*, no. 12 (1962): 183–234.

43. Shatunovskaia, *Ob ushedshem*, 276; Aleksandr Shelepin at *XXII sezd*, vol. 2: 405. For Suslov, see *Istochnik*, no. 2 (1996): 115.

44. Rybakov, *Roman*, 177.

45. See Larina, *This I Cannot Forget*, 240–46; and Roy Medvedev in Cohen, ed., *An End*, 119–23.

46. Ardov, et al., *Legendarnaia Ordynka*, 259; Zezina, *Sovetskaia khudozhestvennaia*, 174; and, similarly, Koen, *Dolgoe*, 104.

47. Ibid.

48. Mikhail Sokolov in *Current Digest of the Soviet Press*, April 24, 1963: 13; Ivan Lazutin, *Sud idet* (Moscow, 1962), 258.

49. *Khrushchev: dva tsveta*, vol. 2: 581. For his "readiness," see Anna Akhmatova quoted in Joshua Rubenstein, *Tangled Loyalties* (New York, 1996), 249.

50. See the exchange between Ehrenburg and Viktor Yermilov in *Izvestiia*, Jan. 30 and Feb. 6, 1963; for Khrushchev, Taubman, *Khrushchev*, 596; the anonymous letter from a Russian writer in *Encounter*, June 1964: 88–98; and Leonid Ilyichev in *Current Digest*, April 3, 1963: 6.

51. *Politicheskii dnevnik*, vol. 2 (Amsterdam, 1975): 123. Several suggestive articles about fascist Germany were written by Yevgeny Gnedin. See *Novyi mir*, no. 3 (1966), and no. 8 (1968). For other examples, see Koen, *Dolgoe*, 104–05.

52. Khrushchev, *Khrushchev*, 14.

53. For Shatunovskaya, Snegov, and Aksyonov, see her *Ob ushedshem*, chaps. 20–23; Khrushchev, *Khrushchev*, 15; and Aksyonov in *Novaia gazeta*, July 8, 2009. For Leningrad, see Dobson, *Khrushchev's Cold Summer*, 54, 87.

54. Shatunovskaia, *Ob ushedshem*, 292; and Semichastnyi, *Bespokoinoe*, 161.

55. *Pravda*, Oct. 21, 1962. For Khrushchev, see Evgenii Evtushenko, *Volchii pasport* (Moscow, 1998), 241–43.

56. Andrei Karaulev, *Vokrug kremlia* (Moscow, 1990), 50.

57. Fedor Burlatsky, *Khrushchev and the First Russian Spring* (New York, 1988), 200–01, 215; Pavlov, *Anastas Mikoian*, 314–19; G.L. Smirnov in *Neizvestnaia Rossiia*, vol. 3 (Moscow, 1993): 377–81; and Semichastnyi, *Bespokoinoe*, 342–43. For the summary report, see *Reabilitatsiia*, vol. 2: 541–670.

58. *Nikita Khrushchev 1964*.

59. Rybakov, *Roman*, 41.

60. *Current Digest*, Feb. 5, 1964; Evtushenko, *Volchii pasport*, 242; and *Current Digest*, Aug. 5, 1964: 20.

61. See, respectively, Saraskina, *Aleksandr Solzhenitsyn*, 525; Taubman, *Khrushchev*, 14, and, similarly, *Nikita Khrushchev 1964*, 211, 340, 346, 347; and *Istochnik*, no. 2 (1996): 115.

62. Saraskina, *Aleksandr Solzhenitsyn*, 535; O. Volin in *Sovershenno sekretno*, no. 6 (1989): 18; Ulanovskaia and Ulanovskaia, *Istoriia*, 269.

Chapter 5

1. This section on the Stalin question, reformers, and conservatives draws on my 1985 book *Rethinking*, chaps. 4–5, and on a forthcoming expanded version of that book.

2. Feliks Chuyev in Cohen, ed., *An End*, 174.

3. For examples of these complaints, see, respectively, *Preduprezhdenie pravonarushenii sredi nesovershennoletnikh* (Minsk, 1969), 12; and Cohen, *Rethinking*, 200 n. 77.

4. Quoted in *The New York Times*, Dec. 3, 1978.

5. Rudolf L. Tokés, ed., *Dissent in the USSR* (Baltimore, 1975), 351.

6. See the interview with Karpinsky in Stephen F. Cohen and Katrina vanden Heuvel, *Voices of Glasnost* (New York, 1989), 280–306.

7.   Pyotr Pospelov in *Vsesoiuznoe soveshchanie*, 298; and *Khronika zashchity prav v SSSR* (New York), July–Sept. 1977: 16–17.

8.   For Molotov's account, see *Molotov Remembers*, 409–11; and for Chernenko's, *Reabilitatsiia*, vol. 2: 538–59.

9.   *Kremlevskii samosud* (Moscow, 1994), 209–11, 361; *Reabilitatsiia*, vol. 2: 539–40; Semichastnyi, *Bespokoinoe*, 245.

10.   Tepliakov, *Protsedura*, 64; and Lidiia Golovkova in *Novaia gazeta*, Dec. 16, 2009.

11.   Lev Sheinin, *Zapiski sledovatelia* (Moscow, 1968); and the obituary in *Izvestiia*, May 31, 1967. For his role in the terror, see Zviagentsev, *Rudenko*, 73–78, and the relevant pages in Vaksberg, *Stalin's Prosecutor*; and for the quote, Valerii Rodos, *Ia—syn palacha* (Moscow, 2008), 29.

12.   *Izvestiia*, Dec. 16, 1963.

13.   See Medvedev, *Khrushchev*, 98, for a somewhat different version; and Solzhenitsyn, *Gulag*, vol. 3: 451.

14.   A returnee quoted in Adler, *Gulag Survivor*, 196–197. For Snegov and Suslov, see *Reabilitatsiia*, vol. 2: 510, 521–25; and for appealing to Snegov (and Shatunovskaya), Orlova and Kopelev, *My zhili*, 53.

15.   See, e.g., Roy Medvedev, *On Socialist Democracy* (New York, 1975).

16.   Larina, *This I Cannot Forget*, 343–45. Similarly, see Yuri Tomsky in Proskurin, ed., *Vozvrashchennye imena*, vol. 2: 270.

17.   Tatiana Rybakova, *"Schastlivaia ty, Tania!"* (Moscow, 2005), 255; and Khrushchev quoted in Philip Boobbyer, *Conscience, Dissent and Reform in Soviet Russia* (London, 2005), 66.

18.   *Nikita Khrushchev 1964*, 441. For Viktor Louis's life, see Elena Korenevskaia in *Literaturnaia gazeta*, Feb. 10–16, 2010.

19.   Khrushchev, *Vremia. Liudu. Vlast*, vol. 1: 163.

20.   Iuliu Edlis in *Sovetskaia kultura*, Dec. 21, 1989; and Orlova and Kopelev, *My zhili*, 347–348.

21.   L.P. Petrovskii, *Petr Petrovskii* (Alma-Ata, 1974); Anton Rakitin, *V.A. Antonov-Ovseenko* (Moscow, 1975).

22. For a translation, see Mikhail Shatrov, *Dramas of the Revolution* (Moscow, 1990).

23. Quoted in Woll, *Invented Truth*, 14.

24. *Otblesk kostra.*

25. For representative writings and other documents in this evolution, see George Saunders, ed., *Samizdat* (New York, 1974); Abraham Brumberg, ed., *In Quest of Justice* (New York, 1970); and Cohen, ed., *An End to Silence.*

26. Larina, *This I Cannot Forget*, 183. For a sympathetic account of Yakir's life by his son-in-law, Yuli Kim, from which I take some of this information, see *Obshchaia gazeta*, Feb. 8–14, 1996; and, similarly, Leonid Petrovskii in *Kentavr*, no. 1 (1995): 61–75.

27. L.N. Dzhrnazian in *Sotsiologicheskie issledovania*, no. 5 (1988): 64.

28. M.S. Gorbachev, *Izbrannye rechi i stati*, 7 vols. (Moscow, 1987–1990), vol. 5: 217, 397–98, 401–02, 407. For Yeltsin, see *Svobodnaia mysl*, no. 11 (1995): 62–63.

29. G.A. Bordiugov and V.A. Kozlov, *Istoriia i koniunktura* (Moscow, 1992), chap. 2.

30. See, e.g., Proskurin, ed., *Vozvrashchennye imena*, 2 vols.; and F.A. Karmanov and S.A. Panov, eds., *Reabilitirovan posmertno*, 2 vols. (Moscow, 1988). For "sluice gates," see Anatoly Chernyaev, *My Six Years with Gorbachev* (University Park, PA, 2000), 139.

31. Nanci Adler, *Victims of Soviet Terror* (Westport, CT, 1993).

32. *Delo.*

33. *The Nation*, April 17, 1989: 521–24.

34. Quoted by Iurii Shchekochikhin in *Literaturnaia gazeta*, July 6, 1988.

35. For the meetings, see *Foreign Broadcast Information Service: Soviet Union*, Sept. 14, 1990: 24; and *Izvestiia*, Aug. 25, 1989. For more on Krayushkin, who later was instrumental in providing information about the fates of famous Soviet writers, see Shentalinsky, *Arrested Voices.*

36. The lists began appearing in 1990 in *Vecherniaia Moskva*, and later were the basis of three expanded volumes published by the Memorial Society under the title *Rasstrelnye spiski* in 1993, 1995, and 2000. For a revealing interview with Milchakov, see David Remnick, *Lenin's Tomb* (New York, 1993), 137–40.

37. See, e.g., *Moscow News*, nos. 19, 28, 42 (1988), and nos. 10, 37 (1990); and *Komsomolskaia pravda*, Dec. 8, 1989. For the editor, see Vitaly Korotich quoted by G.Z. Ioffe in *Otechestvennaia istoriia*, no. 4 (2002): 164; and, similarly, Koen, *Dolgoe*, 107. For the remorse, see Rudolf Syisask in "Pravda GULAGa," *Novaia gazeta*, March 3, 2010.

38. *Nedelia*, Dec. 26–31, 1988; and on a symbolic trial, Koen, *Dolgoe*, 107.

39. *Literaturnaia gazeta*, March 29, 1989.

40. Larina, *This I Cannot Forget*, 339.

41. Quoted by N.B. Ivanova in *Gorbachevskie chteniia*, no. 4 (2006): 81. Similarly, see Koen, *Dolgoe*, 107.

42. See the letter in *Izvestiia*, May 7, 1992.

43. *Komsomolskaia pravda*, Sept. 26, 1990.

Epilogue

1. See, e.g., the VTsIOM survey in *Johnson's Russia List* (hereafter *JRL*), an email newsletter, Dec. 21, 2009; A.V. Filippov, *Noveishaia istoriia Rossii, 1945–2006 gg.* (Moscow, 2007), 93; and A.T. Rybin, *Stalin v oktiabre 1941 g.* (Moscow, 1995), 5.

2. Aleksandr Bovin, who comments similarly in Cohen and vanden Heuvel, *Voices*, 225.

3. *Reabilitatsiia*, vol. 3: 600–06; and Adler, *Gulag Survivor*, 33 and chap.7.

4. *Dva sledstvennykh dela*, 3.

5. For the 1990s, see Stephen F. Cohen, *Failed Crusade*, expanded ed. (New York, 2001).

6.   B.S. in *Nezavisimaia gazeta*, Sept. 21, 1993; and, similarly, *Mir posle Gulaga*.

7.   Sergei Cherniakhovskii and, on the same point, Aleksandr Bangerskii in *Politicheskii klass*, Dec. 2009, online ed.; earlier n. 1; and Sarah E. Mendelson and Theodore P. Gerber in *Foreign Affairs*, Jan./Feb. 2006, online ed.

8.   Wendy Slater in *The Times Literary Supplement*, Oct. 30, 2009: 29; and, similarly, *The Economist*, Sept. 5, 2009: 14.

9.   See, e.g., Iurii Mukhin and Aleksandr Shabalov, *Pochemu vrut uchebniki istorii* (Moscow, 2009).

10.   See, e.g., *Novaia gazeta*, March 16, April 22, and July 29, 2009.

11.   See, e.g., the two volumes edited by Irina Shcherbakova, *Kak nashikh dedov zabirali* and *Krug semi i koleso istorii* (Moscow, 2007 and 2008).

12.   For Pozner, see the BBC report in *JRL*, Dec. 23, 2009; and for the documentary, *Novaia gazeta*, Jan. 25, 2010.

13.   For the court decision, see ibid., Oct. 16, 2009; for Magadan, ITAR-TASS report, May 23, 2008, and, similarly, AP dispatch in *JRL*, July 9, 2007.

14.   For the quote, see N.B. Ivanova in *Gorbachevskie chteniia*, no. 4: 81; and for the memorial, *Novaia gazeta*, June 5–8 and 9–15, 2008, and the Communist Party press releases opposing it on June 5–6, 2008.

15.   Filippov, *Noveishaia*, 81–94. Protests against government support for the book and related teacher manuals appeared in *Novaia gazeta* regularly in 2008 and 2009.

16.   See, respectively, Reuters dispatch, Nov. 2, 2000; *Knizhnoe obozrenie*, no. 48 (2006): 4; and kremlin.ru, Oct. 30, 2007, along with the ITAR-TASS report the same day.

17.   AFP dispatch in *JRL*, Feb. 4, 2010; and for Putin's words, quoted by ITAR-TASS, ibid., Dec. 22. 2009.

18.   *Izvestiia*, Dec. 1, 1990.

19. See, respectively, Vladimir Ryzhkov in *Moscow Times*, Feb. 9, 2010; Aleksandra Samarina in *Nezavisimaia gazeta*, Nov. 2, 2009; and, similarly, Aleksandr Budberg in *Moskovskii komsomolets*, Dec. 28, 2009.

20. See, respectively, Mikhail Delyagin quoted by Sergei Mitrofanov, Polit.ru, Jan. 3, 2010; the roundtable discussion in *Zavtra*, Dec. 31, 2009; and Aleksandr Prokhanov in *Zavtra*, March 4, 2009. Similarly, see Iurii Mukhin, *Stalin protiv krizisa* (Moscow, 2009).

21. See, respectively, Sergei Chernyakhovsky in *Moscow News*, Dec. 1–7, 2009; Rybin, *Stalin*, 5; Vladimir Karpov quoted by Zhanna Kasianenko in *Sovetskaia Rossiia*, July 27, 2002; and Mikhail Anokhin in *Literaturnaia gazeta*, March 18–24, 2009.

22. *Novaia gazeta*, July 1, 2009.

23. Andrei Fefelov quoted by Edmund Griffiths in *The Times Literary Supplement*, Jan. 30, 2009: 14. The other quote on the first page of this chapter, from Aleksandr Sergeyev, is also cited by Griffiths.

24. See, e.g., Gennadii Ziuganov, *Stalin i sovremennost* (Moscow, 2008); Iurii Emelianov, *Stalin pered sudom pigmeev* (Moscow, 2007); and the voluminous coverage of the one hundred and thirtieth anniversary of Stalin's birth, in December 2009, in the pro-Communist newspaper *Sovetskaia Rossiia*.

25. The expression is Aleksandr Budberg's, in *Moskovskii komsomolets*, Dec. 28, 2009. For my analysis at that time, see Cohen, ed., *An End*, 22–50; and my *Rethinking*, especially chaps. 4–5.

26. *Delo*, 256. For the poll, see Paul Goble in *JRL*, Feb. 24, 2006. For examples of grandchildren, see earlier, n. 11.

27. For the meeting, see Dmitrii Muratov in *Novaia gazeta*, Feb. 2, 2009; and his interview with RFE/RL in *JRL*, Jan. 30, 2009. For Medvedev quoted in this paragraph and the next, see blog.kremlin.ru, Oct. 30, 2009.

Index

A

Adler, Nanci, 23
Aikhenvald, Yuri, 15, *53*
    allusions of, 137
    post-release life of, 61–62
    stigma of, 61
Akhmatova, Anna, 29, 57, 81–82, 173
    on Khrushchev, 152
Aksyonov, Pavel, 19, 69, *117*
Aksyonov, Vasily, 19, 24, 29, 92, *117*
    citizenship of, 21
    false information about, 109
    on his mother, 69
    on reading secret files, 169
Aldan-Semyonov, Andrei, 137
All Roads Lead to Vorkuta (Negretov), 41
Amis, Martin, 24
amnesty
    government, 33
    partial, 36
Andropov, Yuri, 21, 140
anketa (personal questionnaire), 30
anonymous Russian-language
        questionnaire, 20
anti-Stalinists, 170–172
Antonov-Ovseyenko, Anton, 12, 58,
        121, *156*, *166*
    apartment search of, 21
    capabilities of, 13–14
    on forbidden truth, 96
    sister of, 68
    writings of, 89, 137, 145
Antonov-Ovseyenko, Vladimir, 90–91
Arosev, Aleksandr, 68
Aroseva, Olga, 68–69
    career of, 30–31

Molotov and, 83
arrested property, 74–76
Article 58, 4, 35. *See also*
        counterrevolutionaries
Astrov, Valentin, 149

B

Baitalsky, Mikhail, 15
    memoirs of, 95
    views of, 133–134
Ballod, Inge, *120*, *157*
Bayev, Aleksandr, 14, 59, 81, 88
Bayeva, Tatyana (Tanya), 14, *122*, 135,
        141
    dissident activities of, 14, 59
    emigration of, 133
Berggolts, Olga, 62–63, 64
Beria, Lavrenti, 4, *49*
    conviction of, 99
    rape by, 34, 36
    trials of, 93
Beria's gang, 99, 145
big zone, 85
Bitov, Andrei, 24
Blyukher, Vasily, 69
Bonner, Yelena, 69, 91
    mother of, 70
book confiscation, 21
Brezhnev, Leonid, 87
    actions of, 108–109
    burial of, 141
    complaints of, 130
    policies of, 127
    reign of, 126, 136
    stabilization by, 127–128
Budyonny, Marshal Semyon, 71